educational
technology
for the
global village

educational
technology
for the
global village

worldwide innovation and best practices

Edited by
Les Lloyd and Gabriel I. Barreneche

Information Today, Inc.

Medford, New Jersey

First printing, 2014

Educational Technology for the Global Village: Worldwide Innovation and Best Practices

Library of Congress Cataloging-in-Publication Data

Lloyd, Les.
  Educational technology for the global village : worldwide innovation and best practices / Les Lloyd and Gabriel I. Barreneche.
      pages cm
  Includes bibliographical references and index.
  ISBN 978-1-57387-481-6
  1. Educational technology--Cross-cultural studies. 2. Education and globalization. I. Title.
  LB1028.3.L62 2014
  371.33--dc 3

                                                                        2013049298

Printed and bound in the United States of America.

President and CEO: Thomas H. Hogan, Sr.
Editor-in-Chief and Publisher: John B. Bryans
Production Manager: Norma J. Neimeister
Managing Editor: Amy M. Reeve
Book Designer: Kara Mia Jalkowski
Cover Designer: Lisa Conroy

infotoday.com

I dedicate this book to Roy, a friend and mentor, whose innovative Spanish for the Professors program taught me enough Spanish (and gave me enough confidence) to dare to bring that first group of students to Mexico and continue venturing out for the past decade. To Scott and Gabriel, who endured several student adventures (also known as service-learning trips) with me as we all learned our way, I am humbled by your patience (with me and with students), your humility, and your skills, and I am grateful for your friendship.

—LL

I dedicate this book to my loving wife Ileana. I could have never gotten this far without your inspiration and support to see this project to its fruition. To my son Mateo, I hope that you will one day be a part of special projects like the ones in these pages. To all of my students, past and present, I thank you for always teaching me something new and challenging me to seek out new paths.

—GIB

Contents

Preface

I have worked in higher education information technology (IT) at some outstanding colleges and universities for longer than I care to remember. I am a traveler. I love getting out of my comfort zone and exploring new areas, meeting new people, and learning about new places. And I like to help people. For many years, I tried to figure out how to meld my IT background and my interest in travel—specifically, how to be a part of the growing interest in study and service abroad. In 2003, it struck me. We were disposing of a large number of computers that were no longer usable at my college. We had done a good job using them until they were no longer practical (at least 5 years). But I knew that there were many areas in the world where computing equipment was not available to students. So here is how I brought everything together:

1. We could take the computers to a school outside the United States.

2. College students could set up the computers and teach the students there how to use them.

3. The college students could also help teach English to the same students to whom they were teaching computer skills.

I came up with a proposal to teach a freshman seminar class both web skills and Spanish and Mexican history and culture, and together we would travel during the 10 days before Christmas to complete our task: teaching middle school-aged students how to use computers, leaving them with enough computers to continue their studies. That is where my foray into this decade-long project began.

In a similar fashion to my initial thought process of how to combine IT and travel, after that first trip was over, I began work on a book that would both document what we had experienced and function as a template for others to do similar work. It took another 7 years to come up with a topic that was deemed publishable, hence the creation of this book.

—Les Lloyd

This project represents the marriage of two of my professional passions: instructional technology and global learning. As a professor of Spanish, I have found instructional technology to be an indispensable part of my approach to teaching foreign language. Students readily respond to the authentic interaction that technology facilitates in the language classroom, and they can learn so much about the people and culture whose languages they are learning through this computer-mediated communication. Although one of the ideal ways for students to learn language and culture is through immersion in the language through study abroad or community engagement activities, today's technology can serve as a viable alternative when these travel experiences are not feasible.

Through the case study I detail in Chapter 1 of this text, I was able to personally witness the important role that technology can play in teaching students about the complexities of our world and how these experiences can prepare them for life in the "global village," beyond language learning. Years later, this book project gives us the opportunity to see how colleagues in other disciplines across the country have integrated technology and learning in the global context, and to integrate these ideas and best practices in future projects at our home institutions.

—Gabriel I. Barreneche

Introduction

Although the editors of and contributors to *Educational Technology for the Global Village* come from a broad spectrum of academic fields and specializations, the common bond they share is a keen insight into how to use today's educational technology in a way that both enhances student learning and contributes to global understanding. The chapters in this anthology highlight best practices in educational technology and how it can be used to enhance internationalization efforts. The editors have included projects that explore how the use of technology both in the United States and abroad can impact student learning, and how that technology can bring together people from different corners of the globe. We also aim to demonstrate different models of interaction and communication: from face-to-face technological exchanges to asynchronous and live computer-mediated communication. Our hope is that the chapters included in this anthology can serve as templates that readers can apply to their specific areas of expertise and instruction.

Our contributors' projects reflect the varied terrain of access to the world of technology and the challenges facing different segments of our global village. On one hand, we see that access to the web and web interface tools presents few problems in developed and technologically advanced countries, such as South Korea and Spain. On the other hand, in the developing world, the digital divide would appear to be insurmountable but for the efforts of our contributors in remote corners of Asia, Africa, Latin America, and the Caribbean. Through the examples presented in this text, however, we see clearly the power of communication and instant access to the world of the web and the importance of sharing technology and technological know-how. This is an important lesson for students and instructors alike.

Finally, a number of technologies are discussed as being educational or instructional, including Facebook, Skype, Second Life, and the iPad.

Clearly this is not their only function. However, we have discussed how these mainstream technologies can be used for educational purposes.

The possibilities afforded by instructional technology to build bridges between the diverse peoples of the world seem endless. As educators in this globalized and technology-filled environment, our task is to find the most effective ways to guide our students across those bridges and make sense of the interconnectedness afforded by that technology. We trust that this collection of works will facilitate discussions among colleagues and inspire new and creative applications of instructional technology, with the aim of raising intercultural awareness among our students and preparing them for the challenges of a living in a global village.

CHAPTER 1

Learning Global Citizenship Through Teaching Technology

Gabriel I. Barreneche

As technology and interconnectivity bring people of the world in ever closer contact, institutions of higher education look to educate tomorrow's global citizens, preparing them for the challenges and opportunities of this new landscape. While technological advances such as the internet, Skype, mobile telephones, and wireless connectivity are making the world "smaller" by eliminating barriers to instantaneous communication, it is not clear what the moral response to this smaller world should be for citizens who are privileged to have access to this technology. When technological skills and knowledge are shared with those on the other side of the digital divide, what is learned by the instructor/donor? In other words, through the experience of teaching technology, what can the teachers learn from the students about globalization and responsible citizenship?

This chapter will explore how new movements in higher education toward citizenship education, service-learning, and global awareness can intersect with and augment movements in global technology education. By analyzing a case study from an international service-learning project, we shall see that technology can serve as a valuable tool in educating college and university students about global issues of poverty, education, and the digital divide. Additionally, through these types of international service projects, focused on technology education, students can gain the interpersonal, problem-solving, and intercultural skills necessary to thrive and succeed in the global marketplace. Finally, the results of this case study will demonstrate that this type of international service technology teaching project can assist institutions of higher education in achieving their goals of educating students for global awareness and citizenship.

Service-Learning Theory and Praxis in Higher Education

Over the past two decades, institutions of higher education have been making use of community-based learning and service-learning pedagogy to engage their students and serve the greater good of the communities in which they are located. This movement toward greater student involvement in community issues and service has its roots in the theories of engaged learning developed by John Dewey (1942) and Paulo Freire (1970). Before entering into a detailed discussion of the service movement in higher education, it is important to have a clear understanding of the terminology that is being used. Service-learning researchers Robert Bringle and Julie Hatcher (1995) clearly define service-learning as follows:

> We consider service-learning to be a course-based, credit-bearing educational experience in which students (a) participate in an organized service activity that meets identified community needs and (b) reflect on the service activity in such a way as to gain further understanding of the course content, a broader appreciation of the discipline, and an enhanced sense of civic responsibility. This is in contrast to cocurricular and extracurricular service, from which learning may occur, but for which there is no formal evaluation and documentation of academic learning. (112)

It is important to note the distinction that Bringle and Hatcher make between community service and service-learning. The course-based learning objectives linked to the service activity are what distinguish service-learning from the numerous cocurricular and extracurricular service and volunteer activities found on campuses and throughout the greater community. Another way of distinguishing service-learning from other service activities is to determine if the particular academic course would be significantly different in its achievement of learning objectives if the service activity were not present. In simpler terms, service-learning is one of many teaching tools that educators can employ in achieving the learning objectives of a given academic course. Janet Eyler and Dwight Giles argue in their 1999 book *Where's the Learning in Service-Learning?* that, in service-learning, both the service and learning goals are primary in the course and must be clearly linked to one another.

A broader term used frequently to identify academic activities that engage students outside of the classroom is community-based learning (CBL). In contrast to service-learning, in which students generally are working to address a specific need identified by the community partner, CBL activities are not necessarily directly related to service. An example of a CBL activity would be language students participating in conversation exchanges with native speakers of the target language from the local community. While the learning activity takes place in the local community (and outside of the classroom), these linguistic exchanges do not necessarily address a community partner's need. For the purposes of this chapter, we will be closely examining the narrower field of service-learning rather than CBL.

Over the years, service-learning pedagogy has become more formalized, and its contributions to higher education have been better documented, thanks to the work of numerous researchers in the field. These efforts have been spearheaded by a combination of college and university faculty in conjunction with national service organizations such as the National Service-Learning Clearinghouse/Campus Compact, peer-reviewed research publications such as the *Michigan Journal of Community Service-Learning*, and annual conferences such as the one hosted by the International Association for Research on Service-Learning and Community Engagement. In order to formalize and standardize community-based learning practices at the institutional level, the Carnegie Foundation for the Advancement of Teaching offers a Community Engagement Classification (classifications.carnegie foundation.org/descriptions/community_engagement.php), which provides colleges and universities with frameworks and criteria so that their curricular objectives align with their service-learning efforts. In doing so, the Carnegie Classification recognizes the academic legitimacy and value of this type of pedagogy. Finally, colleges and universities have made efforts to standardize their community engagement practices by designating specific service-learning and/or community engagement courses as such. In doing so, faculty must adhere to certain norms and best practices; students then have prior knowledge of the expectations of the courses in which they enroll. Examples of institutions with these academic service-learning norms include Rollins College, the University of Georgia, and the University of Central Florida.

In addition to the benefits gained by the community partners in having student volunteers making contributions to their organizations, research has shown that these course-based activities have positive impacts on student learning. For example, the research of Alexander Astin and colleagues (2000) demonstrates increased learning outcomes in student writing, while Patricia Fredericksen (2000) shows that student performance in class improved through service-learning. Research has demonstrated increased development of students' cognitive skills and academic motivation (Bringle, Phillips, and Hudson 2004) through service-learning. Eyler and Giles (1999) also observe increased motivation in students to learn the course material because of a direct connection to the service-learning project in addition to improved problem-solving skills and higher levels of complex thinking (75). Furthermore, the authors note an increased development of critical thinking skills through high-level service-learning experiences (101). However, Eyler and Giles caution that one must consider the fact that the cognitive development of the student can influence the level of these gains. The results of these and numerous other research projects on the benefits of service-learning clearly underscore the academic nature of this type of experiential pedagogy.

Educating Students for Active and Responsible Citizenship

Beyond having a positive effect on student learning and motivation, service-learning also assists faculty and the broader institution in achieving the goal of educating students for active and responsible citizenship. Colleges and universities around the country have dedicated valuable and scarce resources to the establishment of centers for community engagement and service in the hopes of educating students on the importance of participating in the community and becoming active members of society. This emphasis on education with a focus on creating positive outcomes for society is not new to the higher education landscape. Educational theoretician Ernest Boyer argues that, beyond the individualistic goals of career and personal interest, higher education must instill in students a sense of responsibility to their community

(1987, 67–68) and that institutions of higher education have a duty to connect their vast resources with social issues and transform the campus into "staging grounds for action" for solving these problems (1996, 32). This emphasis on citizenship and community engagement can be seen more recently in the National Leadership Council for Liberal Education and America's Promise's (LEAP) 2007 report "College Learning for the New Global Century." According to this report, one of the four essential learning outcomes for students today is "personal and social responsibility, including civic knowledge and engagement—local and global, intercultural knowledge and competence, ethical reasoning and action, and foundations and skills for lifelong learning (anchored through active involvement with diverse communities and real-world challenges)" (3) (Figure 1.1).

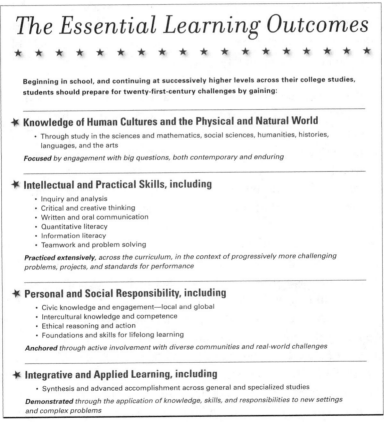

Figure 1.1   The essential learning outcomes from the LEAP report (www.aacu.org/leap)

Academic service-learning and community-based learning can serve as vehicles for institutions of higher education to achieve these learning outcomes for today's student. According to Astin and colleagues (2000), among the outcomes for students in service-learning courses are a heightened sense of civic responsibility and an increased likelihood of pursuing a career in a service field after graduation. Similarly, Eyler and Giles (1999) maintain that service-learning leads to engagement, connection, and active citizenship (157). By linking theory on what it means for students to become active and responsible members of their communities with hands-on activities outside of the classroom, educators make the course material relevant to the students and achieve the improved learning outcomes discussed earlier.

On the other hand, this increased involvement of institutions of higher education through community engagement activities has not always been the norm. According to Boyer and Arthur Levine (1981), higher education has vacillated between focusing on preparing students for their vocation and career and the institution's greater social obligation to the broader community:

> Each general education revival moved in the direction of community and away from social fragmentation. The focus consistently has been on shared values, shared responsibilities, shared governance, a shared heritage, and a shared world vision. To us, this is an important point. It suggests that the ebb and flow of general education is, in fact, a mirror of broader shifts in the nation's mood. (17)

Now, more than 30 years since Boyer and Levine's study, our nation's mood can be characterized as one of institutions of higher education and their students actively looking to share and engage with the local community. College and university students today are more likely to come to campus with experience and interest in volunteering and serving the community. According to the U.S. Bureau of Labor Statistics (2012), 22.6 percent of people aged 16 to 24 volunteered in the year 2012. The Corporation for National and Community Service (2006) also reports that, "In 2005, approximately 30.2 percent of college students volunteered, exceeding the volunteer rate for the general adult population of 28.8 percent" (2). In sum, today's college-aged students are generally interested and experienced in community engagement, providing fertile ground for academic service-learning courses and initiatives across college and university campuses.

Globalizing the Curriculum

There is no arguing that today's students need to prepare for an ever more interconnected and globalized society. It is not enough to simply educate students for success in their region or state; they must graduate with the skills and abilities to thrive in the competitive global marketplace. Higher education is keenly aware that a 21st-century education requires that students achieve certain intercultural competencies and a general awareness of the world beyond our borders. For example, according to Nelly Furman, David Goldberg, and Natalie Lusin's Modern Language Association report (2010), enrollments in the study of languages other than English at institutions of higher education reached a new high in 2009, including a notable increase in enrollments in the languages outside of the 15 most commonly taught languages. In addition to increased study of foreign languages, more and more students are participating in international educational experiences during their college years. For example, according to the Institute of International Education's "Open Doors Report on International Educational Exchange" (2012), over 273,000 university students from the U.S. studied abroad for academic credit during academic year 2010–2011, more than triple the number of students from two decades before.

As well as international travel experiences, colleges and universities are providing valuable global perspectives through initiatives to internationalize their faculty and curriculum. In discussing a study by the International Association of Universities, Aisha Labi (2009) explains that the primary objective for internationalization efforts across higher education has shifted from a focus on research to a focus on preparing students for a globalized society:

> Strengthening research capacity through international collaborations, which in 2005 ranked second in importance only to internationalizing the faculty and student body, is no longer among the top three rationales institutions cite for why they are internationalizing. Instead, their current priorities, in order of importance, are improving student preparedness,

internationalizing their curricula, and enhancing their institution's international profile and reputation.

On the faculty side of the equation, institutions are not just encouraging their students to participate in study abroad programs. For example,
at Rollins College, in Winter Park, Florida, home to the author and this
study, every 3 years faculty members qualify for an internationalization
grant to travel to a country they have never visited before as part of
an educational tour or research trip. The objective of this grant is that
faculty return to campus and share their global experiences with their
students through new additions to the courses they teach.

In addition to a more globalized curriculum and focus on international issues and challenges, student travel abroad, in various forms,
contributes to the global consciousness that is now an increasingly
prevalent learning objective. International experiences for students can
take the form of traditional study abroad at a host institution in a foreign
country, short-term immersion experiences led by a faculty member
from the student's home institution, noncredit cocurricular experiences
of short or intermediate duration, and longer-term internships abroad,
among others.

While all of these experiences have merit in advancing global learning objectives, international trips with a service-learning focus can
achieve both the global awareness objective and also the personal and
social responsibility outcomes that the LEAP learning report argues
for, as discussed earlier. Bringle and Hatcher (2011) go so far as to
claim that "International service-learning [ISL] ... may be a pedagogy
that is best suited to prepare college graduates to be active global
citizens in the 21st century," (3) and that the field of international
service-learning lies at the triple intersection of the educational domains
of international education, study abroad, and service-learning (4). They
further define ISL as follows:

> A structured academic experience in another country in
> which students (a) participate in an organized service activ-
> ity that addresses identified community needs; (b) learn
> from direct interaction and cross-cultural dialogue with
> others; and (c) reflect on the experience in such a way as
> to gain further understanding of course content, a deeper
> understanding of global and intercultural issues, a broader

appreciation of the host country and the discipline, and an enhanced sense of their own responsibilities as citizens, locally and globally. (19)

The increasing demand for such learning experiences that take students beyond classroom learning can be seen in the proliferation of service-oriented trip offerings from both colleges and universities as well as from international study service providers, such as IPSL and Amizade International, among others. One must be cautious, however, in the structure and delivery of such international service-oriented experiences for students. Following the best practices of service-learning generally, educators and organizers of international service trips must be mindful of developing equal, respectful, and reciprocal relationships with the community partner abroad (Eyler and Giles 1999) and to not replicate colonialist/imperialist structures in the service project (Kahn 2011). Organizers must be very careful as well in not placing the community partner in any position that can be detrimental to their group and must adhere to a policy of "do no harm."

Case Study: The World Wide Web in Mexico

The following case study will illustrate how the institutional goals of global citizenship and personal and social responsibility can be achieved through an international academic service-learning experience focused on bridging the digital divide globally.

In 2003 and 2004, the associate vice president of information technology at Rollins College organized an international academic service-learning experience for first-year students called The World Wide Web in Mexico. Although the focus of this case study will be the 2003 and 2004 experiences, similar iterations of this project took place from 2005 to 2009 with service trips to Cuenca and Galapagos, Ecuador, and the Bahamian island of Abaco. Assisting the associate vice president in 2003 and 2004 were two Rollins faculty members—one from the department of education to assist with lesson planning and pedagogy, and one from the Spanish program to conduct the language component of the course. Also, during the 2004 project, a group of Rollins students developed a basic English language program for the Mexican students in addition to the computer skills course that was piloted the previous year. Additional details about this project can be found in Chapter 12.

Preservice Seminar

As part of their first-year seminar, called the Rollins College Conference (RCC), students in The World Wide Web in Mexico seminars in 2003 and 2004 designed, prepared, and implemented a curriculum to teach webpage design and computer literacy to underprivileged elementary school students near the town of San Miguel de Allende in Central Mexico. The objective of the preservice course was for students to learn about Mexican culture, history, society, and the digital divide in a developing country, in addition to developing global awareness through service to others. Over the course of the semester, students also engaged in readings about Mexico, the economic and social effects of the North American Free Trade Agreement, and Mexican immigration to the United States. In preparation for December's service-learning trip after the completion of final exams, the RCC students created and executed fundraising activities to collect money to purchase the used laptop computers that would be used for instruction in Mexico, and eventually donated to the partner schools. The students collaborated in groups to create a curriculum for 5 days of computer instruction, while also learning about social and economic issues in modern Mexico and Spanish technology-based vocabulary and conversational Spanish. Prior to departure, the students also produced instructional guides in English and Spanish that would be left with the partner schools' administrators and teachers so that they could continue to effectively use and maintain the computers that the Rollins group was donating.

It is important to note that, in working with students in the first semester of their first year of college, the expectation at the end of the course was not that they would immediately be transformed into global civil servants ready to tackle all of the social problems of the world. A developmental approach to student learning can result in a deeper and more long-lasting impact. In other words, one isolated service-learning experience will not achieve all of the desired learning outcomes in civic knowledge and global awareness. Eyler and Giles explain that, "the principle of continuity was central to Dewey's thinking; learning is never finished but is a lifelong process of understanding" (1999, 183). They also contend that, although high-level service-learning contributes to the development of critical thinking skills, students experience more significant cognitive development through multiple service experiences (125).

Service-Learning Trip

Over the course of the week of instruction, Rollins students were placed at two schools in the San Miguel de Allende area, each with differing levels of computer literacy and English competency, ranging from absolute zero to intermediate-level competency (Figure 1.2). For many of the Mexican students, especially in the more rural school, it was the first time they had ever used a personal computer. As such, the curriculum designed by the Rollins students provided (in Spanish) a complete overview of the parts and workings of a laptop computer. While the initial aim of the 2003 groups was to train the Mexican children on web design, limited access to a reliable internet connection forced the group to change strategy and focus. The plans for teaching Microsoft FrontPage, a WYSIWYG HTML editor and website administration tool, were scrapped, and the Rollins students created a new curriculum teaching PowerPoint and Publisher, as well as word processing software so that the Mexican children could create school newsletters and disseminate information in a new way with their families and

Figure 1.2   A Rollins student assisting young Mexican students with basic computer skills

community. This technical hiccup provided the students a valuable lesson in being flexible and improvising one's plans under challenging circumstances.

At the end of 5 days of intense instruction at the local schools, the Mexican students were able to create presentations and newsletters for their families and community. They also learned how to take pictures using digital cameras (which were also donated to the schools), upload the pictures from the cameras to the laptops, and then use them in the digital media they were producing. The students were eager to share their new knowledge of computers with their families and created letters and cards with images, different fonts, colors, and formatting. One of the local schools was procuring funds and materials to build a computer lab where the students could put their new computers and computing knowledge to use as part of their academic learning.

Keeping in mind the importance of developing respectful and reciprocal relationships, the group of students from Rollins did not come to the schools with the hierarchical mindset of simply imparting their knowledge and leaving behind some computers. The group was sensitive to the need to develop a trusting relationship with the Mexican students and their teachers. In order to accomplish this goal, the group organized games and ice-breaker activities with the children and engaged in linguistic exchanges with them so as to improve their Spanish skills (Figure 1.3).

This personal interaction with the Mexican children and their teachers addressed the course goal of developing intercultural competence and enhancing the Rollins students' global perspective. At the end of

Figure 1.3   Mexican students participating in an ice-breaker activity
          with a Rollins student

the week of instruction, all of the community schools where the Rollins group was working held ceremonies and thank you *fiestas*. The families wanted to demonstrate their gratitude and share their cultural customs with an authentic Christmas party, complete with piñatas, *aguinaldos* (small, handmade "goodie bags" with holiday candies), homemade food, games, and music. At these farewell celebrations, the close bond between the Rollins students and their Mexican counterparts was most evident. Speeches were made, gifts exchanged, and even a few tears shed. By the end of the week of service, it was clear that the Rollins group had learned and received more from the Mexican students than they had given in computing and English instruction.

Impact of the Experience

As with any well-designed service-learning project, the students were required to submit an extensive reflection assignment in the days following their return from Mexico. In these reflections, one can clearly see how the computer education project for the Mexican students turned into a citizenship and global awareness lesson for the Rollins students. For reasons of privacy, the names of the students will not be revealed. One student remarked:

> When I first signed up for this course, I didn't really know what to expect. … I signed up because I thought it would be interesting. I was completely unaware as to how the trip to Mexico would completely change my outlook on life.

Another student commented about the experience of teaching:

> It made me see that one of my obligations [in] being fortunate enough to have the opportunities that I do is to continue giving to those less fortunate. It wasn't until that [last] day at the school that I realized this.

As discussed earlier, one experience will not forever change a student's perspective, but it will set him on a path for further exploration and discovery. After graduation, the following student went on to pursue legal studies:

> After spending 5 days with the students from Campana, I really felt that I was a changed person. The impact that we all had on their lives was immeasurable, and that changed me in a way that I cannot describe. I learned that the things that matter most in life are those things that impact the lives of others.

This sentiment of altruism and a call to service to the global community is also echoed in the following reflection:

> Being able to teach students in a different setting than what I am used to just refocused [me] and made me confident that being an educator is what I want to do. I'd like to change the world (who wouldn't?), and I hope that with more experiences like this one and the chance to keep improving myself while at the same time helping and giving back to others, I will be able to continue this type of work while exploring more worlds.

Finally, a student who had previously demonstrated a passion for social issues found his values and ideals validated by the experience:

> This trip was not only moving and motivational to me, but it again reaffirmed my dreams of being a social worker and eventually my dream of changing the world in the magnitude of Marx, MLK, Gandhi, and Che Guevara. Even though we were able to touch the lives of only so few, I have to believe that even if we changed the life of one of those students that our trip was well worth our while.

Much of the deep impact that these projects had on the students can be attributed to their working though situations beyond their usual comfort zones, both physical and emotional. A colleague of the author refers to the importance of a "squirm and learn" approach to service-learning. In other words, when students are challenged to move beyond what is familiar and safe for them, they are more actively engaged in their learning and will exceed the limits of what they already know. The first challenge that pushed the students outside of their comfort zones was climatic. The weather in San Miguel in mid-December is typically cool during the day and chilly in the evenings, oftentimes close to freezing. Our accommodations during both of these trips did not have central heat or a readily available supply of hot water to accommodate a group as large as ours. Although there were numerous complaints about the living arrangements at first, the students quickly adapted to the more difficult conditions and focused on the project at hand. Secondly, although a few students were native speakers of Spanish or had high linguistic competency before the trip, the majority experienced difficulties in communicating with our Mexican counterparts as well as with the children, most of whom spoke absolutely no English. The linguistic obstacles presented by not having sufficient Spanish skills further pushed the students out of their comfort zones and challenged them to find other means of interpersonal communication. The intralingual negotiation between the students and our hosts yielded a deeper appreciation of the challenges immigrants with limited English skills face in our own country. However, one must be cautious in challenging students to go beyond the realm of the familiar in a travel abroad environment. If pushed too far and too soon, students may revolt and counteract the positive outcomes of the experience for the rest of the group.

The long-term impact of service-learning experiences beyond graduation from undergraduate studies is an area that warrants further research. Anecdotally, years after the 2003 and 2004 trips to Mexico, several of the participants are currently working in or continuing studies in fields related to international study and service. One participant is currently completing a PhD program in Spanish language and literature. Another received a master of social work from Columbia University, focusing on the juvenile system, and will shortly begin law school. This same student wrote a senior thesis at Rollins on the experience of young Mexican migrants in the Central Florida area. One of the 2004 participants is working as an international admissions counselor at a college in the Northeast. Finally, a 2003 participant spent a semester studying abroad in Spain and has channeled his international experiences into founding his own Spanish wine importing company.

Conclusion

As seen by the case study presented, technology teaching can be a valuable vehicle for educating our students about global issues and the need for social action. Students learn valuable intercultural, problem solving, and leadership skills while developing sensitivity to other cultures and peoples through close, meaningful, and positive interactions with the host country. By having students "serve and learn" during an international experience, they gain an international perspective beyond experiencing the other through the "tourist gaze." Technology education in an international setting can bridge the gaps between cultures while empowering both the students who impart the skills and the students who receive the valuable training. Furthermore, technology education can be at the center of a critical triple intersection, international education, study abroad, and service-learning, as Bringle and Hatcher suggest. This is not to suggest that every college and university should rush out to implement an international technology-based service-learning program. Such educational experiences must be carefully designed, articulated, and executed in deliberate and culturally sensitive ways following the best practices of service-learning pedagogy and academic study abroad. In doing so, a particular course's learning objectives can be realized along with the institution's global outreach and citizenship goals. Finally, just as technology connects people across countries and continents, teaching people how to use technology through an international service-learning program can connect and transform all those involved.

References

Astin, Alexander W., Lori J. Vogelgesang, Elaine K. Ikeda, and Jennifer A. Yee. 2000. *How Service Learning Affects Students.* Los Angeles: University of California, Higher Education Research Institute. heri.ucla.edu/pdfs/rhowas.pdf.

Boyer, Ernest L. 1987. *College: The Undergraduate Experience in America.* New York: Harper.

———. 1996. "Stated Meeting Report: The Scholarship of Engagement." *Bulletin of the American Academy of Arts and Sciences* 49(7): 18–33.

Boyer, Ernest L., and Arthur Levine. 1981. *A Quest for Common Learning (The Aims of Higher Education: A Carnegie Foundation Essay).* Washington, DC: The Carnegie Foundation for the Advancement of Teaching.

Bringle, Robert G., and Julie A. Hatcher. 1995. "A Service-Learning Curriculum for Faculty." *Michigan Journal of Community Service-Learning* 2(1): 112–122.

———. 2011. "International Service Learning." In *International Service Learning: Conceptual Frameworks and Research*, edited by Robert G. Bringle, Julie A. Hatcher, and Steven G. Jones, 3–28. Sterling, VA: Stylus Publishing.

Bringle, Robert G., Mindy A. Phillips, and Michael Hudson. 2004. *The Measure of Service Learning: Research Scales to Assess Student Experiences.* Washington, DC: American Psychological Association.

Corporation for National and Community Service. 2006. "College Students Helping America: Executive Summary." www.nationalservice.gov/pdf/06_1016_RPD_college_full.pdf.

Dewey, John. 1942. *Democracy and Education: An Introduction to the Philosophy of Education.* New York: Macmillan.

Eyler, Janet S. and Dwight E. Giles, Jr. 1999. *Where's the Learning in Service-Learning?* San Francisco: Jossey-Bass.

Fredericksen, Patricia J. 2000. "Does Service Learning Make a Difference in Student Performance?" *Journal of Experiential Education* 23(2): 64–74.

Freire, Paulo. 1970. *Pedagogy of the Oppressed.* Translated by Myra Bergman Ramos. New York: Herder.

Furman, Nelly, David Goldberg, and Natalia Lusin. 2010. "Enrollments in Languages Other Than English in United States Institutions of Higher Education, Fall 2009." Modern Language Association of America. www.mla.org/pdf/2009_enrollment_survey.pdf.

Institute of International Education. 2012. "Open Doors Report on International Educational Exchange." www.iie.org/Research-and-Publications/Publications-and-Reports/IIE-Bookstore/Open-Doors-2012.

Kahn, Hilary E. 2011. "Overcoming the Challenges of International Service Learning." In *International Service Learning: Conceptual Frameworks and Research*, edited by Robert G. Bringle, Julie A. Hatcher, and Steven G. Jones, 113–124. Sterling, VA: Stylus Publishing.

Labi, Aisha. 2009. "Priorities in Internationalization Shift From Research to Preparing Students." *Chronicle of Higher Education* (September 20). chronicle.com/article/Internalizations-Focus/48530.

National Leadership Council for Liberal Education and America's Promise. 2007. *College Learning for the New Global Century.* Washington, DC: AACU. www.aacu.org/leap/documents/GlobalCentury_final.pdf.

U.S. Bureau of Labor Statistics. 2012. "Volunteering in the United States." www.bls.gov/news.release/volun.nr0.htm.

CHAPTER 2

Service-Learning Linked to Social Media and Virtual Worlds: An Educational Strategy for Promoting Global Sustainability

Brian Shmaefsky

Contemporary computer-based virtual worlds and social media primarily serve as recreational ways of interacting for entertainment or personal communication. There have been many recent attempts to use virtual worlds and social media as an educational technology with varying degrees of effectiveness. Educational technology can supplement many aspects of teaching, including civic awareness, environmental sustainability, and global awareness.

This chapter presents a model on how service-learning can be blended with virtual worlds and social media to effectively teach students how to participate actively in shaping a sustainable future. Virtual worlds and social media are educational technologies that provide students with improved opportunities to take part in global sustainable changes. Service-learning blended with educational technologies present faculty with an innovative higher education strategy that encourages a high degree of participation by students in various components of the curriculum. In addition, this strategy is a measurable and reliable vehicle for institutional change toward improved participation in community and global development.

The student-driven project began when Lone Star College–Kingwood general biology and environmental geology students used a virtual world environment and social media to design and evaluate an integrated

19

waste and water management model involving wastewater use, bio-digesters, and rainwater catchment systems for a newly built Gawad Kalinga (GK) village in Batangas, Philippines. GK describes itself as a "Philippine-based movement that aims to end poverty by first restoring the dignity of the poor. It employs an integrated and holistic approach to empowerment with values formation and leadership development at its core." During the project, students investigated ways by which developing nations can conserve water, use wastewater and sewage, and reduce mosquito-borne diseases. The project evolved on-site to include improvements to the local school and community center for the village. Plus, the project is being expanded to Colombia and Honduras.

Virtual Worlds and Social Media in Instruction

Global communication and personal interaction are changing dramatically due to the new types of connectivity provided by the internet, including easy and quick access to information from around the world and the reduction of effort and time needed to investigate global events. The ability to communicate globally at a reasonable cost is another benefit of the internet. Education has taken advantage of the internet in many ways to improve teaching and facilitate student-directed instruction.

In this study, students made use of Second Life, a virtual world designed for typically synchronous social networking, and Facebook, the current standard in asynchronous social networking. Second Life permits educators and students to build virtual environments that serve the same purpose as resource libraries, lectures, and project workstations. The workstations can be used to share a wide array of projects, ranging from clothing design to urban development plans.

Facebook has become a valuable educational medium because it is inexpensive to use and does not require high-end graphics capabilities that might not be available at schools. Current classroom uses include creating project workgroups, scheduling events and project meetings, sending messages, sharing media and other resources, posting class notes, discussing issues, and facilitating student connectivity.

Students in the project made use of Second Life and Facebook based on the communication capabilities of partners assisting in the project and of stakeholders in the Philippines. The students accomplished this by assessing the computing capabilities of all of the people involved in the project.

The Second Life virtual village for the project contained a learning center about the project, a virtual library of references, and a model system that could be manipulated based on feedback from all of the stakeholders. In the early stages of the project, the Second Life village was used by the student groups to share designs about the sustainable water system models with group members and with faculty and local volunteer consultants. Later in the project, faculty from the University of the Philippines and volunteers with GK were provided with the model projects through the Second Life website for further feedback. Villagers in the GK houses were then shown the approved models for further feedback, and these became the systems that were built by the villagers.

The Facebook page set up for the class evolved to play a different role in the project. At first, it was set up mainly for communication; it was simpler and quicker to share comments and photographs through Facebook. Plus, many people could be invited to comment on the project as it was evolving. Later, the Facebook page evolved into a means of disseminating the project to other students and organizations interested in carrying out similar projects. Plus, it was more feasible for villagers in other GK villages to share the information through Facebook at local internet cafés.

Service-Learning as an Instructional Strategy

Service-learning is best described as an experiential learning method that enriches learning by engaging students in meaningful service to their academic institutions and local or global communities. Students involved in service-learning apply academic skills to solving real-world issues, linking established learning objectives with genuine needs. They lead this process, with the help of faculty and community partners, by applying critical thinking and problem-solving skills to social issues such as animal welfare, environmental justice, ethnic intolerance, malnutrition, natural disaster recovery, natural resource conservation, and poverty.

It is well-documented that college courses that use service-learning instructional approaches improve retention of course material and promote civic duty awareness. Service-learning reinforces course content by involving students in volunteer community development activities that apply what they learned in class. Meaningful community service with instruction and reflection enriches the learning experience, teaches civic responsibility, and strengthens local and global communities. Service-learning combines community service with classroom instruction. It focuses on critical, reflective thinking as well as personal and civic responsibility. Service-learning programs involve students in activities that address community needs while developing their academic skills and commitment to community contribution.

Authentic service-learning experiences have been identified to possess certain characteristics, according to the National Service-Learning Clearinghouse in the United States:

- Service-learning experiences are positive, meaningful, and real to the student participants.

- Projects involve cooperative rather than competitive experiences and promote a variety of skills associated with citizenship, community involvement, and teamwork.

- Service-learning projects address complex problems in realistic settings rather than simplified problems in isolation.

- The projects offer opportunities to engage in problem-solving by requiring students to gain knowledge of the specific context of their service-learning activity and community challenges, rather than only to draw upon generalized or abstract knowledge, such as that which might come from a textbook. As a result, service-learning offers powerful opportunities to develop critical thinking strategies.

- Service-learning participation promotes deeper learning because the results are immediate and uncontrived. As a result of this immediacy of experience, service-learning is more likely to be personally meaningful to students. The experiences generate emotional responses and challenge values as well as ideas. Thus, it supports social, emotional, and cognitive learning and development.

In this study, service-learning, in combination with virtual world and social media, was used to reinforce the principles of biology, geology, global natural resources, and sustainability through volunteer activities for resolving an international water resource need.

Global Sustainability Awareness

Sustainability is now recognized by international development organizations, such as the United Nations and the International Bank for Reconstruction and Development, as the only rational way to build societies that use human and natural resources responsibly. The concept of sustainability is an important and multifaceted topic of discussion for the higher education community. Higher education institutions need to embrace sustainable development as an essential topic within the classroom as well as a model for environmental and social sustainability. Colleges need to encourage students and the community they serve to recognize that global quality of life can be achieved through sustainability. They can foster sustainability by expanding student and community awareness of how to create a more healthy and equitable world for all people. In addition, academic institutions can be the incubator for driving creative problem-solving through hands-on experimentation using student and community input.

The curriculum components for sustainability characteristically have the following student-learning outcomes:

- Uses real and virtual experiences to gain knowledge of sustainability issues

- Stimulates ownership and responsibility in personal and everyday actions as well as social actions and decisions within the community

- Empowers students to evaluate their actions and helps them make more consistent decisions that benefit all beings

- Increases critical thinking skills and deep problem-solving by using cyclical reasoning and real-world examples to better understand class subject matter

The goal of building a sustainability culture is to encourage students as citizens to anticipate and prevent problems rather than following the unsuccessful model of trying to react and fix unmaintainable situations after they occur. Sustainability education also teaches that future accounting processes associated with economic and social development must reflect all long-term environmental and economic costs and may not be consistent with those practices of the current market. It also shows people how to make the best decisions based on sound, accurate, and up-to-date information. Effective sustainability education demonstrates how to live off the environment in a manner that provides for and does not destroy its capital base. Another sustainability value is that the quality of social and economic development must take precedence over the mere acquisitions or the quantity of resources. Lastly, a sustainability culture instills a respect for nature and the rights of future generations.

Academic institutions can use their current infrastructure to build in a sustainability component for educating students and the public. Many colleges and universities already promote sound economic development and celebrate the cultural diversity needed to build sustainable societies. They can use their science programs to increase the biological diversity and complexity of the ecosystems locally and globally. At the same time, academic institutions can use the resources of their arts, humanities, and social sciences programs to plan stabilized populations and resource consumption at a level that is within the carrying capacity of local and global ecosystems.

It is well-recognized in the higher education literature that sustainability education is a long-term effort that transforms students and the community at all levels in order to promote a mindset change necessary to achieve an accurate and coherent vision. Higher education has the influence to be a leader in building a sustainable future by exercising its role in training the next generation of community leaders, professionals, and teachers who will guide the insights and policies needed to face the challenges of rebuilding a society willing to live equitably and conserve natural resources.

An underlying philosophy of sustainable education is that it is not merely a concept taught in the same manner as any other subject in the classroom. The facts making up sustainability principles are only the bricks and mortar that build the infrastructure. Students and the community cannot just be told to memorize principles of sustainable development. They need to experience and work within a model sustainable situation. Academic institutions must provide a dynamic learning environment in which to explore what a sustainable lifestyle means. The model must place students and community members in an environment with the following attributes:

- A social mindset that gives hope for a future with a healthy environment, a strong economy, and an equitable society

- An intellectual climate that gives people an understanding of the important role each individual plays in designing and creating a sustainable future

- Experiences that allow people to work directly with their entire community, including educators, government officials, community members, and the business community

- A learning environment that effectively combines engaging and relevant content with high-quality pedagogical strategies

Service-learning integrated into educational technologies, social media, and virtual environments is a natural pedagogical tool for building a global sustainability education program that educates students and community members according to the criteria previously discussed. It can be used as a supplement for individual courses, a capstone project for a degree program, or a hands-on component of community training workshops.

Building a Global Sustainability Education Curriculum

The original purpose of the project described earlier was to add an international education component to the science coursework at Lone Star College–Kingwood. Internationalization of the curriculum was prioritized by the college leadership as an essential feature of a workforce ready to graduate. Plus, students needed to be prepared for the growing influence of other countries on lifestyles in the United States. The faculty involved in the project decided to select sustainable development as the focus of the international component because it was an emerging global ideology for future economic and social growth. At the time the project was planned, the college students worked on local environmental and social sustainability issues in the Houston area through programs coordinated by the service-learning office. In these local activities, students assisted nonprofit and nongovernmental agencies on local sustainability issues ranging from environmental justice to stakeholder water quality issues.

The international endeavor accomplished in this project was carried out by environmental geology and introductory biology students over a 2-year period. It was intended to be a student-directed project with faculty, expert consultants, and stakeholders acting as facilitators. Learning outcomes were identified for the classes with the hope of designing a model for teaching students the following sustainable development skills:

- How to integrate science concepts with social issues

- How to design appropriate civic responsibility volunteer programs

- How to assess factors that contribute to poverty and social strife

- How to design universal models for resolving local and global societal issues

It was hoped that the model would also show students how to resolve the problems of the effects of natural disasters on people, lifestyles, economy, and resources.

In the first year, all of the students were divided into teams that researched the sustainable water quality needs of the villages in the Philippines. This topic was selected because both classes were studying water quality issues. In addition, each class was learning about local sustainability issues. The teams in the introductory biology course were assigned to research different aspects of current water resources in the Philippines. Each group's charge was to find an issue and then identify low-cost strategies for resolving the issue that were applicable to the resources found in the Philippines. First-year students in the environmental geology class were divided into different types of teams than the introductory biology students. One team assessed and selected the water quality remediation strategies researched by the introductory biology students. The other team built prototypes of the projects and formulated ways to communicate their ideas to the stakeholders in the Philippines.

The stakeholder in the Philippines was the nonprofit humanitarian agency GK. Students made contact with GK through a local group called the Humble/Kingwood; together the groups were known as Humble/Kingwood Gawad Kalinga (HKGK). HKGK helped with public awareness, fundraising, and organizational work for the project. It now goes by the name Humble/Kingwood Filipino American Foundation.

The 2-year project period for the students traveling to the Philippines was divided into three phases that each year accomplished the same learning outcomes described previously. Year one consisted of the following phases:

- Phase 1: Students would assist in building the HKGK village, which would consist of 30 homes and a school (Figure 2.1). This experience would help students better understand the living conditions in the stakeholder villages and the water resource needs of the village residents.

- Phase 2: Students would provide stakeholders with opportunities and options to make the HKGK village a sustainable community based on the students' experiences in the village. In Phase 2, students would evaluate and refine the plans that they proposed to solve the water resource issue for the villages identified for the courses.

Students traveling to the Philippines during the second year of the project carried out the final phase:

- Phase 3: Students would use the HKGK village as a "laboratory" for teaching and developing a sustainable community in other countries.

An important part of Phase 3 was for students to use a strategy to effectively and regularly communicate their plans with the stakeholders in the Philippines.

Figure 2.1   Students building a prototype model of the project that will be rendered in Second Life

The HKGK group was an important partner in the project in Phase 1 because it provided local opportunities for service to the GK organization located in the Philippines.

College faculty and local experts on water quality facilitated the students in both classes by providing comments and information resources. Several students in the first-year group traveled to the Philippines to present their ideas and rework the strategies based on stakeholder feedback.

It was planned that feedback collected by the students returning from the Philippines would form the groundwork for the second-year students in the project. A different group of students would gather the information from the first year to build a prototype sustainable water resource system that would ultimately be constructed in the stakeholder village in the Philippines. This was an intentional feature of the project to instill communication and cooperation between teams working asynchronously on a project.

Project Outcomes

The results of the student project were the design of a feasible sustainable integrated waste and water management system capable of producing methane fuel, a curriculum strategy using service-learning as a means of teaching global sustainability needs, and a method of using social media and virtual worlds as a way of communicating ideas with stakeholders in developing nations.

Students used stakeholder input on the research and development plans they carried out during all three phases to finalize a low-cost sustainable integrated waste and water management system using resources from the village. The students gathered project feasibility input in Phase 2 by designing a survey that was read to village stakeholders in Tagalog and English. Phase 2 information was also gathered by interviews with water resource scientists at the University of the Philippines.

Before traveling to the Philippines in Phase 3, students constructed a small-scale model of the sustainable integrated waste and water management system. The model was evaluated by local scientists and shared with stakeholders by building a virtual model on Second Life. The stakeholders viewed Second Life using personal computers at the village community center, internet cafés, or the University of the Philippines. A Facebook page was also created by the students to communicate design changes with the stakeholders.

The final model consisted of three components: 1) a water catchment system that stored rainwater, 2) a blackwater (sewage-contaminated) diversion system, and 3) a graywater (household wastewater) and blackwater remediation system (Figure 2.2). All of the components were made from local materials that were obtained inexpensively or for free. The water catchment system consisted of reused piping that collected rainwater from roofs in the village and collected the water in a reused plastic drum. The plastic drum contained a locally made coconut fiber filter and was sealed to control mosquitoes. Graywater and blackwater for the other components of the system were collected from the drainage system that flowed untreated into a nearby stream. A simple pipe system was used to divert blackwater to a soft plastic holding tank that generated methane gas. A system of valves was used to collect the methane as a source of cooking fuel. The graywater and remaining blackwater was channeled to a naturally occurring reed bed for phytoremediation of body wastes and contaminants. Stakeholders were provided with inexpensive water testing kits to ensure the effectiveness of the wastewater remediation system. The system was constructed using the

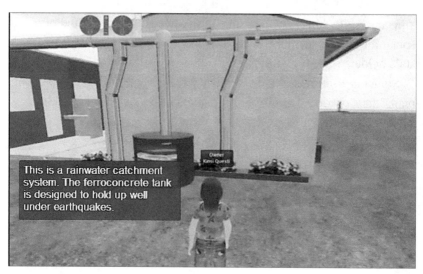

This is a rainwater catchment system. The ferroconcrete tank is designed to hold up well under earthquakes.

Figure 2.2   Final model

virtual model on Second Life and from photographs and specifications shared through Facebook.

Student Evaluation

The learning outcomes of this project were evaluated in several ways:

- Pretest and posttest performance on course content pertinent to the project

- Service-learning preservice and postservice surveys developed by the American Association of Community Colleges

- Evaluation of student presentations about the project by Environmental Protection Agency officials at the 10th Annual P3 Awards: A National Student Design Competition for Sustainability Focusing on People, Prosperity and the Planet, held in Washington, DC, in 2009

- Assessment of project reflections blog posts by students

Overall, this strategy to teach global sustainability significantly improved grades on course content compared to a control population of students. The service-learning preservice and postservice surveys showed that the students significantly improved their attitudes about volunteering for large projects compared to a control population of students.

The results from the National Student Design Competition for Sustainability showed that the students met the following learning outcomes with at least 80 percent performance:

- How to integrate science concepts with social issues

- How to design appropriate civic responsibility volunteer programs

- How to assess factors that contribute to poverty and social strife

- How to design universal models for resolving local and global societal issues

Feedback from students on the project reflections blog posts indicated that students had an overall positive attitude about their involvement in the project and developed a better awareness of global resource issues.

Based on comments from presentations about the project given at several international and national conferences on international education, the project was an effective teaching model because it achieved the following characteristics:

- Integrated science concepts with social issues

- Taught students how to research sustainability models

- Matched appropriate outcomes to a service-learning activity

- Taught students how to assess factors that contribute to poverty and social strife

- Made appropriate use of virtual communication to design universal models for resolving local and global societal issues

- Met the United Nations Educational, Scientific and Cultural Organization (UNESCO) goal of sustainable universities and participation

- Provided students with improved possibilities to take part in sustainable changes

- Fostered innovative methods in higher education characterized by a high degree of participation in the curriculum

- Modeled a vehicle for institutional changes toward improved participation by students

Summary

This was a highly ambitious project, but it can be scaled down to achieve the same outcomes. The project was well-received and perceived as a model for using technology in international service-learning initiatives that build a global village. In addition, dissemination of the project produced partnerships to assist with similar projects in the Philippines and with other developing nations in the future.

The educational technology components of this project provided opportunities for students to use skills and knowledge in real-life situations and extend their learning beyond the classroom and into the global community. Students in the project (Figure 2.3) commented that their use of the educational technology fostered their sense of caring for others locally and globally. They also explained that their use of Second

Figure 2.3 Project team

Life and Facebook components for the project helped them determine and meet real, defined global community needs. The students who did not travel to the Philippines better understood the lifestyles and needs of the project stakeholders through their Second Life and Facebook interactions.

Overall, the project demonstrated that service-learning facilitated by educational technologies promotes the learning of global issues through active participation in service experiences, extends learning about global issues beyond the classroom and into the community, fosters a sense of caring for others locally and globally, and reinforces sustainable planning by encouraging the development of continuing projects having long-term outcomes.

This project also demonstrated its own sustainability because the village stakeholders in the Philippines continue to benefit from the project that is now being carried out by other groups. The project's value and potential for sustainability was further supported when students from the University of the Philippines, participants at the UNESCO International Conference World in Transition: Sustainability Perspectives for Higher Education (San Luis Potosi, Mexico, 5–7 July 2007), and faculty attending a forum on this project at Texas A&M University at Kingsville saw this as a feasible continuing project for their institutions. Plus, funding agencies at the 2009 Reunión Anual de la Asamblea de Gobernadores del Banco Interamericano de Desarrollo y de la Corporación Interamericana de Inversiones in Medellin, Colombia, recommended it as a program for funding in rural communities of Colombia.

In spite of the benefits of the project, there are precautions that must be taken with projects that involve international cooperation and travel. Before attempting a project such as this, the instructor must seek out assistance from nongovernmental agencies in countries proposed for service and must contact local community groups composed of people from those countries. It is also important to consult with others who have had success with similar endeavors, find creative ways for students to seek funding for travel and infrastructure needs (such as virtual world subscriptions), seek funding from foundations that work specifically in the country where you want to do service, and become familiar with the U.S. Department of State travel warnings and consular information sheets. Most important is that students must be briefed on communicating with the culture they are serving.

Acknowledgments

This project was in part funded by the EPA-sponsored P3 Awards: A National Student Design Competition for Sustainability Focusing on People, Prosperity and the Planet (EPA Grant Number: SU833938) and the Lone Star College System Faculty International Explorations Grant. The other grant co-principle investigators—Jason Ford, Cherith M. Letargo, and Jimmi Fischer Rushing—are commended for their tireless efforts in making the project successful for the stakeholders and the students.

Bibliography

Agyeman, Julian. "Human Equality and Environmental Quality." Paper presented at the annual meeting of the North American Association for Environmental Education, Little Rock, AR, October 11–15, 2001.

Bartel, Caroline A., Richard Saavedra, and Linn Van Dyne. "Design Conditions for Learning in Community Service Contexts." *Journal of Organizational Behavior* 22, no. 4 (2001): 367-385.

Beierle, Thomas C., and Jerry Cayford. *Democracy in Practice: Public Participation in Environmental Decisions*. Washington, DC: Resources for the Future, 2002.

Bernard, Anne K. "Education for All 2000 Assessment, Thematic Studies: Education for All and Children Who Are Excluded." Paper presented at the World Education Forum. Dakar, Senegal. April 26–28, 2000.

Bringle Robert G., and Donna K. Duffy. "Collaborating With the Community: Psychology and Service-Learning." In *With Service in Mind: Concepts and Models for Service-Learning in Psychology*, eds. Edward Zlotkowski and Robert G. Bringle (Washington, DC: American Association for Higher Education, 1998).

Bringle, Robert G., and Julie A. Hatcher. "Implementing Service-Learning in Higher Education." *Journal of Higher Education* 67, no. 2 (1996): 221–239.

———. "A Service-Learning Curriculum for Faculty." *Michigan Journal of Community Service-Learning* 2, no. 1 (1995): 112–122.

Carini, Robert M., George D. Kuh, and Stephen P. Klein. "Student Engagement and Student Learning: Testing the Linkages." *Research in Higher Education* 47, 1 (2006): 1–32.

Chang, Yao- Jen, Tsen-Yung Wang, Shu-Fang Chen, and Rhi-Hus Liao. "Student Engineers as Agents of Change: Combining Social Inclusion in the Professional Development of Electrical and Computer Engineering Students." *Systemic Practice and Action Research* 24, no. 3 (2011): 237–245.

Cheal, Catheryn, John Coughlin, and Shaun Moore. *Transformation in Teaching: Social Media Strategies in Higher Education*. Santa Rosa, CA: Informing Science Press, 2012.

Dinçer, Gökhan Deniz. "The Creation of Academic Consulting Environment in Virtual Worlds and an Assessment of Challenges Faced by Learners in this Environment." *eLearning & Software for Education* 1 (2011): 290–296.

Ellison, Nicole B., Charles Steinfield, and Cliff Lampe. "The Benefits of Facebook 'Friends': Exploring the Relationship Between College Students' Use of Online Social Networks and Social Capital." *Journal of Computer-Mediated Communication* 12, no. 4 (2007): 1143–1168.

Fien, John, and Rupert Maclean. "Teacher Education for Sustainability: Two Teacher Education Projects from Asia and the Pacific." *Journal of Science Education and Technology* 9, no. 1 (March 2000): 37–48.

Heyn, Michael, Katrina Lythgoe, and Charles Myers. "Education and Economic Development: Sustainability, Threshold, and Equity." Paper presented at the Third UNESCO-ACEID International Conference on Educational Innovation for Sustainable Development, Bangkok, Thailand, December 1–4, 1997.

Honnet, Ellen Porter, and Susan J. Poulsen. *Principles of Good Practice for Combining Service and Learning: A Wingspread Special Report*. Racine, WA: Johnson Foundation, Inc., 1980.

Hopkins, Charles, Jeanne Damlamian, and Gustavo Lopez Ospina. "Evolving Towards Education for Sustainable Development: An International Perspective." *Nature and Resources* 32, no. 3 (1996): 2–11.

Hopkins, Charles and Rosalyn McKeown. 1999. "Education for Sustainable Development." *Forum for Applied Research and Public Policy* 14, no. 4 (1999): 25–28.

———. "Education for Sustainable Development: An International Perspective." In *Education and Sustainability: Responding to the Global Challenge*, ed. Daniella Tilbury, Robert B. Stevenson, John Fein, and Danie Schreuder, 13–24. (Gland, Switzerland and Cambridge, UK: IUCN Commission on Education and Communication, 2002). ibcperu.org/doc/isis/13028.pdf.

Howard, Jeffrey. "Community Service-Learning in the Curriculum." In *Praxis 1: A Faculty Casebook on Community Service-Learning*, ed. Jeffrey Howard, 3–12. (Ann Arbor, MI: Office of Community Service-learning Press, 1993).

Kendall, Jane C. and Associates, ed. *Combining Service and Learning: A Resource Book for Community and Public Service*. 3 vols. Raleigh, NC: National Society for Internships and Experiential Education, 1990.

Keup, Jennifer R. "The Impact of Curricular Interventions on Intended Second-Year Enrollment." *Journal of College Student Retention* 7, no. 1–2 (2005): 61–89.

Kupiec, Tamar Y. *Rethinking Tradition: Integrating Service With Academic Study on College Campuses*. Providence, RI: Campus Compact, 1993.

McClaren, Milton. "Education, Not Ideology." *Green Teacher Magazine* 35 (1993): 17–18.

―――. "Environmental Literacy. A Critical Element of a Liberal Education for the 21st Century." *Education Manitoba* 17, no. 1 (1989): 168–171.

McKenzie-Mohr, Doug, and William Smith. *Fostering Sustainable Behavior: An Introduction to Community-Based Social Marketing.* Gabriola Island, British Columbia: New Society Publishers, 1999.

Meadows, Donella H. *The Global Citizen.* Washington, DC: Island Press, 1991.

Nigro, Georgia, and Stanton Wortham. "Service-Learning Through Action Research Partnerships." In *With Service in Mind: Concepts and Models for Service-Learning in Psychology*, eds. Edward Zlotkowski and Robert G. Bringle (Washington, DC: American Association for Higher Education, 1998).

Osborne, Randall E., Kenneth Weadick, and James Penticuff. "Service-Learning: From Process to Impact." In *With Service in Mind: Concepts and Models for Service-Learning in Psychology*, eds. Edward Zlotkowski and Robert G. Bringle (Washington, DC: American Association for Higher Education, 1998).

Ramaswami, Rama. "Is There a Second Life for Virtual Worlds?" *Campus Technology Magazine* 25, no. 1 (2011): 24. campustechnology.com/articles/2011/09/01/is-there-a-second-life-for-virtual-worlds.aspx.

Salaway, Gail, and Judith Borreson Caruso. *The ECAR Study of Undergraduate Students and Information Technology.* Boulder, CO: EDUCAUSE Center for Applied Research, 2010.

Selwyn, Neil. "An Investigation of Differences in Undergraduates' Academic Use of the Internet." *Active Learning in Higher Education* 9, no. 1 (2008): 11–22.

Siniscalco, Maria Teresa. "Education for All 2000 Assessment, Thematic Studies: Achieving Education for All; Demographic Challenges." Paper presented at the World Education Forum, Dakar, Senegal, April 26–28, 2000. unesdoc.unesco.org/images/0012/001234/123481e.pdf.

Stevens, Christy R., and Patricia J. Campbell, "Collaborating to Connect Global Citizenship, Information Literacy, and Lifelong Learning in the Global Studies Classroom." *References Services Review* 34, no. 4 (2006): 536–556.

Tilbury, Daniella. "Environmental Education for Sustainability: Defining the New Focus of Environmental Education in the 1990s." *Environmental Education Research* 1, no. 2 (1995): 195–212.

UNESCO. "Educating for a Sustainable Future: A Transdisciplinary Vision for Concerted Action." 1997. www.unesco.org/education/tlsf/mods/theme_a/popups/mod01t05s01.html.

―――. "Education for Sustainable Development Toolkit." 2006. unesdoc.unesco.org/images/0015/001524/152453eo.pdf.

————. *World Education Report: The Right to Education: Towards Education for All through Life.* Paris: UNESCO Publishing, 2000. www.unesco.org/education/information/wer/PDFeng/wholewer.PDF.

Webb, Ed. "Engaging Students With Engaging Tools." *Educause Quarterly* 32, no. 4 (2009): 89.

World Commission on Environment and Development. *Our Common Future.* Oxford, UK: Oxford University Press, 1987. www.un-documents.net/our-common-future.pdf.

CHAPTER 3

A Transglobal Virtual Language Learning Community for ESL and EFL Teachers: Using Skype and PBworks

Patricia Davis-Wiley

> Good evening. Welcome to FL/ESL ED 455: Teaching ESL Methods. It's 7 AM here in South Korea and 5 PM there in Knoxville, Tennessee. In class tonight, we will get to know each other, navigate our course website on Blackboard, verify our respective contact lists in our individual Skype accounts, and, lastly, activate our new accounts on PBworks. Is everyone ready?

This scenario took place on the first day of an evening graduate ESL methods class at this World Language/ESL Education professor's home university. She had the unique opportunity to concurrently teach two graduate pedagogy classes, one in South Korea and the other in East Tennessee. As the students entered their classroom at the University of Tennessee (UT), they were physically greeted by one of the professor's graduate students and virtually welcomed by their instructor via Skype. Thanks to the availability of high-speed internet connectivity on both sides of the globe, Skype and PBworks, and the tech-savvy students (Frydenberg and Andone 2010) who comprised the two groups, this particular cyber-connection and many others throughout the semester were executed relatively seamlessly despite the 14-hour time differential between the two class venues. However, much advance planning and organization were required to establish and nurture this virtual learning community (VLC)[1] between the two groups of graduate students: one in southeastern United States learning how to teach English as a Second Language (ESL), and the other in South Korea, learning how to teach English as a Foreign Language (EFL).

This chapter was not written to suggest a rationale for why web-based collaboration should be used[2] in a world where we find "the necessity for preparing students for the interconnectedness among people and nations that characterizes the world today" (Zong, Wilson, and Quashiga 2008, 199), but rather to serve as a vehicle to chronicle the author's personal journey into this relatively new arena. Specifically, it will describe the background of this unique project; detail the procedures followed by the author for establishing both synchronous (Skype) and asynchronous (PBworks) web connections between two different groups of students, one in East Tennessee and the other in Chuncheon, South Korea; highlight both the successes and challenges of VLCs; and make recommendations to other educators who desire to engage in similar endeavors.

Computer-Mediated Instruction for Dual Course Delivery

Although there is a fair amount of published literature concerning the benefits of computer-mediated instruction (CMI) for L2 (second language) students[3] (Belcher 1999; Cheung 2008; Chun 1994; Dykman and Davis 2008; Kitade 2008), Yim (2011) reports that there is a paucity of studies investigating the efficacy of L2 students matriculated in web-supported courses in which they were paired with native English speakers. Thus, the author anticipated that the project described in this chapter could contribute to this void in the related literature and potentially assist others who would wish to do the same. Additionally, the cyber-connections presented in every chapter in this book, including this one, serve to reinforce the notion that a viable and sustainable conduit to establish international connectivity to the global village can be realized through readily available, cost- and user-friendly educational technologies.

Background of the Project

The author was invited to teach a graduate class entitled "Linguistics in the Elementary Schools" to a group of 11 South Korean English education graduate students at Chuncheon National University of Education (CNUE)[4] during an academic winter break at the university.

She had worked as an adjunct professor at CNUE from 1996–2002, during which time she and her colleagues had taught a series of 2-week, twice-yearly conversational English/pedagogy classes in government-sponsored Intensive English Institutes to Korean elementary school teachers who would be teaching English in the elementary schools in South Korea (Davis-Wiley and Wiley 2001). The notion of returning to CNUE to teach intrigued her but presented a particular logistical challenge in that she was scheduled to teach three graduate courses at UT during the same spring semester, the first part of which overlapped the last 2 weeks of her 3-week course at CNUE. How could she concurrently teach at two universities while being physically located in South Korea without missing any class meetings at UT, which could compromise the delivery of course content? Essentially, teaching the three UT classes while based in Korea presented no major problem, since there was a Blackboard[5] course site management presence for all enrolled students that supported asynchronous delivery of course content. Weekly real-time Skype sessions from Korea by the instructor would also take place during the first 2 hours of each UT-based class. All students would have their laptops opened to the Blackboard course site, allowing the instructor to facilitate class activities as though she were physically conducting the class on her home campus. Additionally, given the fact that the three UT classes were offered on Monday, Tuesday, and Wednesday evenings, the professor would be able to Skype into her UT classes at 7 AM from Korea on those mornings, which would actually be 5 PM the evening before in Tennessee. (All UT classes met in the evenings during the semester.)

All of the necessary logistical plans were in place for UT course delivery, originally only using Blackboard and Skype. However, since some of the content of the UT ESL Methods class was similar to the content to be offered in the Korean Linguistics EFL class, this professor decided to cyberlink the ESL and EFL class groups to establish a virtual collaborative learning community that could potentially mutually benefit all students and that would create a new social venue for learning (as suggested by Bigum and Green 1995). To accomplish this, however, she would need to conduct an informal needs assessment (Graves 1996) for the development of the shared components that would be an integral part of both classes, in order to identify common course goals and class activities[6] that could be respectively delivered to and virtually shared with both groups of students in a common web-based collaborative venue. She would also need to identify the most efficient and effective vehicles to accomplish this.

Profiles of the Two Graduate Courses

The class to be offered at CNUE was designated as a graduate linguistics course, but one that was also intended to incorporate specific EFL pedagogical content for its enrolled in-service elementary school teachers who were the English content teachers in their respective elementary schools in Kangwon Province, South Korea. Of the 11 teachers in this class, all were licensed elementary teachers but only three had been English majors in college. Thus, the level of this group's English proficiency would need to be assessed in order for the instructor to accommodate their linguistic needs both in the actual class in South Korea and also in their potential cyber-collaborative paired work with students at UT. The 11 native English-speaking UT graduate ESL Methods class members consisted of four rising English Language Learning (ELL) teacher interns, one add-on ESL endorsement student, three linguistics majors, and three students who were interested in teaching abroad in the near future.

Course Content for the CNUE–UT Collaborative Learning Community

Some of the identified topics to be delivered in the 3-week CNUE course (Table 3.1) were also purposely scheduled to be presented during the same period of time in the UT class (although the latter class would continue for an additional 3 months).

By doing this, it was projected that both groups of students could potentially share ideas and discuss the same second language theories and pedagogical issues in both asynchronous (via ejournaling on the PBworks intranet website) and synchronous (Skype) sessions. The model created for delivery of this VLC appears in Figure 3.1.

Class Content at CNUE

Each CNUE class centered on a second language theory or topic (e.g., Krashen's Affective Filter; see Krashen 1987) presented by the professor in class and supported by PDF resources and PowerPoint presentations

Table 3.1   Common Topics and Activities for CNUE and UT students

Shared Course Topics
First and second language acquisition theories Language proficiency (rubrics, expectations, and assessment) Psycholinguistics and sociolinguistics Language and its relation to the brain The components of language (including pragmatics, semantics, syntax, structure, phonetics, and phonology) International Phonetic Alphabet (IPA)
CNUE and UT Small Group Work at Individual Campuses
Methods of teaching English Planning and conducting mini peer-teaching EFL/ESL lessons
Collaborative VLC Paired Activities
Skype sessions (documented on PBworks) Ejournaling (hosted on PBworks)

(hyperlinked to those pages on the PBworks site). The students could view and listen to all content simultaneously on the interactive whiteboard in the classroom and/or on their desktops (each student had an assigned computer in class). Later, they could review the same material(s) outside of class. A cultural tidbit (e.g., metric conversion from Celsius to Fahrenheit, an American handshake as a greeting) was also discussed and shared. Then an English sound-of-the-day was demonstrated, practiced by all students in class, and reinforced by embedded site hyperlinks to YouTube songs, rhymes, and tongue twisters.

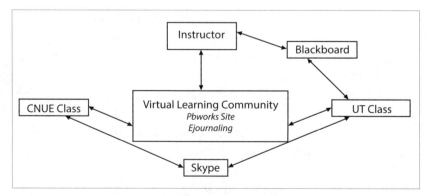

Figure 3.1   VLC model for CNUE and UT classes

In class, the professor would also demonstrate specific activities and materials that could be used in the elementary school English class-rooms, which the CNUE teachers would subsequently practice with partners and then present to the entire class. (All course materials were posted on the CNUE–UT shared PBworks course website.) In the mid-dle of the second week of classes, small teams of students planned and presented mini content-enriched lessons[7] in English to their peers using the students' choice of teaching methods demonstrated and practiced in class. Topics included the same math, health, science, art, and music concepts that were also taught in the Korean schools in Korean.

Almost every day, the CNUE students were assigned a topic for an ejournal entry that was tied into the content offered that day in class. These students were required to ejournal with their assigned UT partner and discuss specific issues, strategies, and materials related to teaching English in a non-English–speaking environment in their PBworks VLC (discussed later in this chapter).

Three web-based vehicles were used to support online collabora-tion between students at CNUE and UT: email, Skype, and PBworks. Since email is a common communicative tool, CNUE and UT students exchanged email addresses before classes started and used this medium primarily to schedule Skype videoconferencing.

Collaboration Using Skype

Many people who have an internet connection and a desire to video- or teleconference with another person outside of their local areas are familiar with Skype (skype.com). The basic Skype membership allows one to virtually link with another Skype user anywhere in the world, using a no-cost download that provides a synchronous (i.e., real-time) connection. A high-speed internet connection and good-quality webcam are important, however, to ensure clear video images, audio connec-tions, and uninterrupted calls.

When the author first planned how she would establish the cyber-learning community that would connect both of her pedagogy classes, she first verified that students at both universities would have the available infra-structures and broadband support for the level of internet connectivity required to establish and maintain the global ties between CNUE and UT. She then asked the English education department at CNUE for the email addresses of her future Korean students in order to communicate with them and ensure that they all had Skype accounts and a working webcam. She then emailed these students to get their Skype names and asked them to send her a Skype contact request in order to schedule a Skype date with them. (The 14-hour time difference created a small challenge that would remain throughout the duration of the project.) During the Skype sessions with the Korean teachers, the professor was able to informally assess their individual English proficiency levels and identify their individual levels of comfort with Skype and other types of computer skills. The students in the ESL Methods class at UT were similarly contacted prior to her departure to South Korea. It was deemed critical to establish a positive rapport with her home university students, albeit via long distance, due to the fact that she would be physically absent for the first three campus meetings. Ben Arbough (2001) stresses the importance of creating and maintaining this positive teacher-student relationship in virtual instructional venues.

Prior to posting permanent American Skype (and ejournal) partners to her Korean teachers on the PBworks site, the instructor introduced her students to Skype videoconferencing etiquette the first day of class in Korea by having a friend from California seemingly "interrupt" her class during its first hour. She dramatically apologized to the class, feigned surprise at the Skype call, and proceeded to chat with the caller for a few moments, explaining that she was in the middle of class in Korea and could not possibly take class time to chat. Her students were so excited about the call that they asked her if they could ask the caller some questions. Over the following 20 minutes, animated two-way conversations took place in which at least half of the 11 CNUE students took turns coming up to the instructor's laptop and engaging in their first Skype conferences with a native English speaker from America (Figure 3.2).

This particular exercise was so successful that the author incorporated at least two Skype calls per week during class time. The CNUE students were prepared ahead of time, however, and had questions to ask the caller, whose identity the professor had announced prior to the Skype call. During these video calls, those students who were not in front of the webcam took notes on questions asked and answers given. Then, following the videoconference (never lasting more than 10 minutes), the students worked in small groups to reconstruct some of the conversations that had taken place on Skype. Summaries were word-processed on the laptop

Figure 3.2   CNUE student (left) conversing via Skype with caller from
            U.S. (right)

of each group's scribe (i.e., designated secretary/recorder) and then
posted to a discussion board on the PBworks website. The professor
then helped the students turn the dialogues into third-person summary
narratives that were then simultaneously projected on the large interactive whiteboard in front of the class. Thus, all four linguistic skills were
practiced during this exercise, and students were able to have firsthand
experience of real-time, live American English in a comfortable and
nonthreatening environment. Following these Skype "adventures," as
they were later called in the class, lists of idiomatic expressions, new
and/or specialized vocabulary, irregular verbs, and unusual sentence
structures were recorded on newsprint that decorated the classroom. By
getting the students comfortable with real-time videoconferencing early
in the 3-week CNUE class, the students became eager to contact their
assigned UT ejournal partners, whom they would Skype twice weekly.

Collaboration Using PBworks

Whereby UT ESL Methods class students were enrolled in a course
website supported by the Blackboard (blackboard.com) online intranet
learning environment at UT, the South Korean students were unable
to interface with the UT students in this course management system
since they were not UT students. Consequently, the author researched
several online options and subsequently selected PBworks (pbworks.
com) to create a free online learning wikispace in which to establish
a cyber-learning community that would also provide a common set
of elearning goals, objectives, and course resources; identify assignments; and host a virtual space for asynchronous communication using

a wiki-based ejournal component. This user-friendly platform allows instructor- controlled access via a web browser (for up to 100 students) using any device connected to the internet. It can also accommodate multimedia audio and video plug-ins and has built-in student accountability, allowing the instructor to view who made which entry and delete or change student entries.

In order to create a free account on PBworks to establish a VLC for her EFL and ESL students, the author went to the PBworks homepage and clicked on Get Started With a Free Version of PBworks Now, then chose the K–12 Education basic option. The entire process took no longer than 2 minutes. Once that was done, she had to organize the virtual environment prior to inviting her Korean and American students to log in to the site.

Organization of the PBworks Website

On the FrontPage of the PBworkspace, there are the following tabs: Pages & Files, Users, and Settings (Figure 3.3). On this page, the author selected the color motif she would use on the site; added her picture; selected different text font styles, colors, and sizes; and welcomed her Korean students to the VLC they would share with their U.S. student partners. She then used the Edit tab to add hyperlinks on the bottom of the page that would assist the students in navigating to different sections of the website (Figure 3.4). PBworks guides the facilitator of the site through each step of this extremely user-friendly process. The site functions similarly to a Word document in its simplicity for text selection and insertion of images and hyperlinks to external websites or simply to other sections (called Pages) of the wiki.

A link to daily activities was listed on the bottom of the FrontPage. Once on the Daily Activities page (Figure 3.5), students could simply click on the Resources link to be connected to PDF files or websites outside of the PBworks intranet VLC (Figure 3.6).

Since the author and her UT students were familiar with Blackboard, she created this wiki site following a similar organization that she used with her UT Blackboard sites. Once the VLC was initially organized, she invited her students from CNUE and UT to join the PBworks space. Thus, both the EFL and ESL teachers were linked to the same intranet VLC, used the same resources from this VLC site, and interacted with

My PBworks   Workspaces   cnue510321   Upgrade Now!

Wiki   Pages & Files   Users   Settings

VIEW   EDIT

FrontPage

last edited by   Dr. Pattie Davis-Wiley 1 year ago   Page history

Dear CNUE Colleagues,
It is my hope that my CNUE graduate students have enjoyed our 3 weeks together in our *Linguistics for Teaching English to Children* class. From my perspective, I have learned a lot working with this talented group of young career professionals who are teaching English to their young students in S.Korea.

My spring 2011 students at The University of Tennessee, Knoxville, where I am Professor of World Languages and ESL Education, have been invited to join this CNUE Intratnet Wiki Website and are engaged in a semester-long journey with their new S. Korean teacher colleagues, during which time, both UT-CNUE partners will Ejournal and SKYPE on a regular basis. It will be my pleasure to facilitate this venture and to maintain the Intratnet environment for this very special project.

All 11 UT FL/ESL 486 ESL Methods students that I am teaching spring 2011 and all 11 CNUE English Ed students in the graduate class I taught between January 3 and January 21, 2001, are actively engaged in this incredible adventure and I wish them well as they learn about each others' cultures, languages and traditions in addition to sharing ideas for teaching their students.

A special reminder to all of my students is that the time in S. Korea is 14 hours *ahead* of Knoxville, TN, so keep that in mind when you make your SKYPE dates! Ejournaling, of course is a 24/7 reality on this wiki website.

I have used a chart like the one below to schedule my own SKYPE sessions with my family and friends:

Korea Time	Knoxville Time
7 a.m.	5 p.m.
8 a.m.	6 p.m.
9 a.m.	7 p.m.
10 a.m.	8 p.m.
11 a.m.	9 p.m.
12 noon	10 p.m.
1 p.m.	11 p.m.
2 p.m.	12 midnight
8 p.m.	6 a.m.
9 p.m.	7 a.m.
10 p.m.	8 a.m.
11 p.m.	9 a.m.
12 midnight	10 a.m.

Figure 3.3   FrontPage of PBworks site

To my UT students: please follow the same directions above and then set up a SKYPE session with your Korean partner as soon as you can.

To both my CNUE and UT students: it is my hope that you will continue both your Ejournaling and SKYPE sessions throughout the spring semester. More soon!

CNUE Syllabus
CNUE Daily Activities
CNUE Mini DemonstrationTeaching Lessons
CNUE Assignments
CNUE Assignment Uploading
CNUE Journals
Miscellaneous
 Resources
UT-CNUE Partner Journals

Figure 3.4   FrontPage hyperlinks to designated sections on the
PBworks site

Daily Activities

last edited by   Dr. Pattie Davis-Wiley 1 year, 11 months ago   Page histor

Date	Topic/Notes	Activity (to be done before class starts on date listed at left)
1-03 M	Introductions Class Overview *Journal assignment #1*	• Our course website is a *wiki* but we will essentially use it as an Intranet environment to view our syllabus, class activities and assignments. We will also use this website to view resources for the class and to upload assignments. • Go to the **Frontpage** and click on the different links on the left side of the page, to navigate through our website! • *Journal Assignment #1*: Click on the **Journals** link, find the initials for your name, click on Edit on top of the page, and then write a brief bio. Once you have done this, click on Insert (horizontal line) and add 2 lines. We will do this each time we make a journal entry. Then, SAVE your work. (The button is on the bottom of the page.) I have done mine as an example for you. My initials are PDW. • *Start reading* **Krashen's Affective Filter** article (also found under **Resources**) . • Needs analysis: what do you want to get out of this class? • Cultural tidbit for the day: conversion of Celsius to Farenheidt (see Resources).
1-04 T	Lang. Acq. Theories and mini lesson plan demo	• We will *start* reviewing Language Acquisition Theories (found under **Resources).** • Components of Language; Cummins' Matrix (found under **Resources** • Review Lesson Plan template to be used in our class (found under **Resources).**

Figure 3.5   Sample Daily Activities page

> ### Songs:
> Row, row, row your boat http://www.youtube.com/watch?v=k50nwLbnDe8&feature=related
> http://www.manythings.org/pp/row_your_boat.html
> The Wheels on the Bus http://www.youtube.com/watch?v=I2dCO3enPfk&feature=related
> If you're happy and you know it http://www.youtube.com/watch?v=lRXsC1J4jJM&feature=related
> http://www.youtube.com/watch?v=yl2AzCsglek&feature=channel
> Head and Shoulders http://www.youtube.com/watch?v=CbknGfQbzhk&feature=related
> The Phonics Song http://www.youtube.com/watch?v=BELIZKpi1Zs&feature=related
> Alphabet Rap (with Elmo from Sesame Street) http://www.youtube.com/watch?v=99WQeH36OZo&feature=related
> Phonics Chant Song http://www.youtube.com/watch?v=JR8n2NyJH8c&feature=channel
> Old McDonald had a farm http://www.youtube.com/watch?v=6_z6zyAe98M&feature=related
> Head, Shoulders, Knees and Toes http://www.youtube.com/watch?v=BisOdUvyoEQ&feature=related
>
> **English Sound System**
> http://www.soundsofenglish.org/pronunciation/index.htm
>
> **Minimal pair drills**
> http://www.manythings.org/pp/
>
> **Pronunciation exercises**
> http://www.eslflow.com/pronunciationlessonplans.html
>
> **English Phonemes**
> http://www.auburn.edu/academic/education/reading_genie/spellings.html
>
> **IPA Chart of the 44 English phonemes (20 vowels and 22 consonants)**
> http://www.esl-lounge.com/pronunciation/phonetic-chart.shtml
>
> **IPA with sounds!**
> http://www.antimoon.com/how/pronunc-soundsipa.htm

Figure 3.6   Sample hyperlinks on Resources page

each other asynchronously on the ejournal section of their shared PBworks workspace.

Ejournaling on the PBworks VLC

As previously mentioned in this chapter, the CNUE students were required to post ejournal entries as part of their daily course assignments. The first entry was an autobiographical one in which the Korean teachers described their academic backgrounds, current teaching assignments, and personal information they felt comfortable sharing with their UT ejournal partners. Many, if not all, first entries included both family and school pictures and descriptions of their schools and teaching assignments (Figure 3.7).

Crystal and Sam's Journal

last edited by   Sehwan Gu 1 year, 9 months ago   Page history

January, 13, 2011.   11:06 pm very very cold ㅠ.ㅠ -18 celsius = - 6 fahrenheit

Hello! nice to meet you. I am Sam.
I live in Wonju, south korea. I am elementary school teacher. My school has only 6 classes. It is very small.
But my school give laptop every student. and we allways do internet everywhere by wireless. Is it cool?
Have you ever been visited south korea? Do you know where korea is on the map?
If you come to korea for traveling, I will help you to have good trip.
I watched TV about heavy snow in New york. Is it ok in Knoxville?
She is my wife Elisabet. I was married Last year. She is also elementary school teacher.
Are you married?
I want to have one son and one daughter, if it is possible.
maybe there is 9 am. have good day! See you SkYPE someday.

Figure 3.7   Example of an initial ejournal entry

The professor assigned a variety of topics, including the challenges of teaching English as a Foreign Language, classroom management issues, favorite teaching strategies, and second language theories and their application to the L2 classroom. Figure 3.8 shows an early ejournal entry from a CNUE elementary EFL teacher.

Journal Assignment #2

The most challenging things when I teach English in my school is as follows :

First, English is not alloted enough in elementary educational curriculum. Childen who are in the third and fourth grade have only two English classes of forty-minute unit a week since 2009, before only one English class a week. That is not sufficient to learn a foreign language well.

Second, English is just one of the nine subjects that are Korean, math, science, P.E., music, art, social studies, ethics, and English. Therefore, I can not pay attention to only English subject.

Third, because I am not a native English speaker, teaching exact pronunciation is almost impossible.

Figure 3.8   Example of a second CNUE ejournal entry

Successes, Challenges, and Recommendations for Establishing a Global VLC

Was the course content for both the ESL and EFL teachers delivered in an effective and efficient way by sharing a VLC PBworks website? The answer is yes. At no time did either group of students express concerns about having difficulty navigating the PBworks site. In fact, they appeared to thrive in this environment, where virtually all class peripherals and resources were accessible in one convenient site. Additionally, both CNUE and UT students reported enjoying the opportunity to communicate and share ideas about teaching, language, food, sports, and culture with each other in the informal ejournals and in Skype conversations. As a result of this cyber-partnership, made possible by the innovative course design described in this chapter, the author witnessed an enhancement of global consciousness in both of her student groups in addition to a subtle transformation of linguistic structures, as evidenced by the written exchanges between the CNUE and UT students. In particular, a serendipitous product of transglobal communication as chronicled in the ejournals was an observable change of tone and structurally complex sentences amongst the CNUE students, from once-stilted, book-learned English to less formal English, using shorter and more concise expressions as well as a liberal use of casual expressions of greeting such as "Wassup" and "Hey." Songül Kilimci (2010) reports that this occurrence is common when different cultures communicate. Several of the students even continued their synchronous virtual (Skype) and asynchronous conversations well beyond the duration of the 3-week CNUE class and after the end of the spring semester at UT. (It should be noted here that there is no apparent time expiration for an established PBworks site, and the author will log in periodically to see if there is any additional activity on the site by the students.)

The major challenge for both sets of students in the VLC was time zone–logistical rather than linguistic. The 14-hour time difference between Korea and Tennessee presented major difficulty for both parties when finding a common time to Skype. Asynchronous ejournaling, by its 24/7 nature, however, was not reported as a problem at any time and was particularly less stressful than Skype conversations, since the students could work at their own pace and "preferred times" (Chen et al. 2007, 217).

Establishing, maintaining, and updating a VLC for any group of students is time-consuming and takes much effort to ensure a seamless delivery to the end users. It is also the responsibility of the VLC's facilitator to ensure that all materials embedded in the VLC are up to date and that the hyperlinks connected to it are still live.

One potential problem with creating a VLC in a global setting is that of internet access for all those connected in the cyber-global village. High-speed internet connectivity is not just a convenience but truly a prerequisite, for the educator who creates a VLC as well as for those who use it as their virtual home. Fortuitously, the venues at both universities involved in the VLC had virtually no problems connecting to and participating in the cyber-environment supported on the PBworks website.[8] Nor did they experience difficulties using Skype or accessing the Web 2.0 software websites. This was not surprising due to the fact that in May 2012, South Korea's broadband network was said to be the fastest (average 17.5 Mbps) and the most developed in the world ("South Korea Retains Internet Speed Crown" 2012). In comparison, the U.S. had an average speed of 5.8 Mbps.

Those who wish to embark upon a journey similar to the author's in their quest to connect global citizens in a cyber-educational community should be encouraged to do so, especially given the fact that the infrastructure support resources are readily available and most importantly, without cost.

Endnotes

1. Yang et al. (2007) define VLCs, or virtual learning communities, as "information technology-based cyberspaces in which individuals and groups of geographically dispersed learners accomplish their goals of elearning" (84).

2. Fish and Gill (2009) and others have already conducted extensive research validating the efficacy of using the internet to enhance the traditional classroom learning environment.

3. Some of the delivery aspects of CMI result in the reduction of students' linguistic pressure, since they can essentially participate outside of the language classroom at their own pace.

4. In South Korea, there are 17 National Universities of Education. CNUE is located in Chuncheon, South Korea, in Kangwon Province.

5. Blackboard is a course site management system used at UT Knoxville. All courses offered at UT have a course website available to the course instructors and enrolled students. The version used at UT offers both asynchronous and synchronous delivery modes.

6. Kathleen Graves suggests that course development should include several components, including a needs assessment, determination of goals, objectives, and organization of course content, class materials, and activities.

7. Lessons were prepared to teach basic math, science, health, geography, and Korean culture content in English at a developmentally, age-, and grade-appropriate level.

8. Kim and Jung (2010) report that the South Korean Ministry of Education, Science, and Technology has made efforts "to create a systemic, technological infrastructure to support an educational system based on advanced information communications technology" (249).

References

Arbough, J. Ben. 2001. "How Instructor Immediacy Behaviors Affect Student Satisfaction and Learning in Web–Based Courses." *Business Communication Quarterly* 64(4): 42–54.

Belcher, Diane D. 1999. "Authentic Interaction in a Virtual Classroom: Leveling the Playing Field in a Graduate Seminar." *Computers and Composition* 16(2): 253–267.

Bigum, Chris, and Bill Green. 1995. *Managing Machines: Educational Administrator and Information Technology.* Geelong: Deakin University Press.

Chen, Yen-Tsu, Liu, Che-Huang, and Roman Wong. 2007. "The Adoption of Synchronous and Asynchronous Media in the Teaching of a Foreign Language." *Issues in Information* 8(1): 217–223.

Cheung, Lisa. 2008. "A Review of the Operation of a Web Bulletin Board in Constructing a Knowledge Building Platform." *Hong Kong Journal of Applied Linguistics* 11(1): 27–44.

Chun, Dorothy M. 1994. "Using Computer Networking to Facilitate the Acquisition of Interactive Competence." *System: An International Journal of Educational Technology and Applied Linguistics* 22(1): 17–31.

Davis-Wiley, Patricia, and Stephen G. Wiley. 2001. "English as Korea's Second Language: Teaching the Teachers How to Teach English in South Korea's Elementary Schools." *International Education* 30(2): 41–49.

Dykman, Charlene A., and Charles K. Davis. 2008. "Online Education Forum: Part Two –Teaching Online Versus Teaching Conventionally." *Journal of Information Systems Education* 19(2): 157–164.

Fish, Wade W., and Peggy B. Gill. 2009. "Perceptions of Online Instruction." *Turkish Online Journal of Educational Technology* 8(1): 53–64.

Frydenberg, Mark, and Diane Andone. 2010. "Two Screens and an Ocean: Collaborating Across Continents and Cultures With Web-Based Tools." *Information System Educational Journal* 8(55): 1–12.

Graves, Kathleen. 1996. *Teachers as Course Developers.* New York: Cambridge University Press.

Kilimci, Songül. 2010. "Integration of the Internet Into a Language Curriculum in a Multicultural Society." *Turkish Online Journal of Educational Technology* 9(1): 107–113.

Kim, Jackie Hee-Young, and Hye-Yoon Jung. 2010. "South Korean Digital Textbook Project." *Computers in the Schools* 27(3–4): 247–265.

Kitade, Keiko. 2008. "The Role of Offline Metalanguage Talk in Asynchronous Computer-Mediated Communication." *Language Learning and Technology* 12(1): 64–84.

Krashen, Stephen. 1987. *Principles and Practice in Second Language Acquisition.* Upper Saddle River, NJ: Prentice Hall International.

"South Korea Retains Internet Speed Crown With 17.5 Mbps." 2012. *Pingdom,* May 2. royal.pingdom.com/2012/05/02/south-korea-internet-speed-17-5-mbps.

Yang, Stephen J.H., Irene Y.L. Chen, Kinshuk, and Niang-Shing Chen. 2007. "Enhancing the Quality of e-Learning in Virtual Learning Communities by Finding Quality Learning Content and Trustworthy Collaborators." *Educational Technology and Society* 10(2): 84–95.

Yim, Yoon-Kyung Kecia. 2011. "Second Language Students' Social Discourse Socialization in Academic Online Communities." *Canadian Modern Language Review/La revue canadienne des langues vivantes* 67(1): 1–27.

Zong, Guinchon, Angene H. Wilson, and Yao Quashiga. 2008. "Global Education: Teaching Social Studies From a Global Perspective: Theory and Research." In *Handbook of Research in Social Education*, edited by Linda S. Levstik and Cynthia A. Tyson, 197–216. New York: Routledge.

CHAPTER 4

Using Asynchronous Web 2.0 Tools to Promote Language Learning and Intercultural Communication

Lina Lee

In today's networked global world, the need for second language (L2) learners to develop intercultural communicative skills has been strongly advocated as an essential component in L2 instruction. According to Byram (1997), intercultural communicative competence (ICC) encompasses a constantly evolving process of developing cultural knowledge, skills of discovery and interaction with others, open attitudes, and critical awareness. It is clear that formal classroom instruction alone is not sufficient to develop learners' ICC. Social interaction with native speakers (NS) through intercultural exchange affords students opportunities to develop their awareness and understanding of other cultures. When face-to-face interaction is not possible, efforts have been made to use computer-mediated communication (CMC) for intercultural collaboration (Belz 2003; O'Dowd and Ritter 2006; Ware and Kramsch 2005). In the last two decades, L2 research across different CMC conditions has been conducted, and compelling findings have been reported in edited collections (Belz and Thorne 2006; Guth and Helm 2010; Levy and Stockwell 2006; O'Dowd 2007). During intercultural interaction, L2 learners gain linguistic and sociolinguistic skills (Kinginger and Belz 2005; Lee 2004, 2008; O'Dowd and Ware 2008; Sauro 2009) and develop cross-cultural awareness through critical reflection (Hauck 2007; Lee 2011, 2012; O'Dowd 2007). For example, the results of the intercultural exchange project conducted by Carney (2009) show that the students of Japanese produced distinct communication skills

57

through various types of CMC, including blogs, wikis, audio, and video chats. Another study conducted by Li Jin and Tony Erben (2007) reveals that the students of Chinese developed greater intercultural sensitivity and showed respect for cultural differences through an online exchange via instant messenger. The process of analyzing and reflecting on native informants' perspectives enables students as outsiders to learn about the cultural framework governing the what, how, and why of insiders' expressions in everyday interactions.

Language and Intercultural Learning With Web 2.0 Technologies

The increased popularity of emerging technologies has continued to shape the field of L2 instruction and research. Among other Web 2.0 tools, blogs and podcasts have received substantial attention from language practitioners (Ducate and Lomicka 2008; Lee 2009; Pinkman 2005; Richardson 2010; Stanley 2006). Web 2.0 technologies offer language learners greater learning opportunities through interaction, collaboration, and community-building beyond the traditional classroom setting. Through social networking, students are exposed to authentic materials and audiences. To date, L2 researchers have carried out cross-cultural exchange projects using various online tools within a wide range of learning contexts. For instance, Lyceum, a software program for audio-graphic conferencing developed by the Open University in the U.K. (Hauck and Youngs 2008), and eTwinning, a method of online networking used in European schools (Miguela 2007), have been developed for intercultural learning. Each web tool has its unique technical features and pedagogical values. The following is an overview of three Web 2.0 tools that have been progressively implemented in L2 learning to foster the development of language skills and promote intercultural learning.

Blogging

Blogs are websites typically authored by an individual and organized in a reverse chronological order over a period of time. Using freely available websites, such as Blogger (blogger.com), WordPress (word press.com), and Edublogs (edublogs.org), anyone can easily create and publish their work on the internet. Unlike static webpages, blogs evolve into a dynamic and interactive network, where authors not only create and update content but also share and exchange ideas through responses with comments (Lee 2010; Richardson 2010). L2 blogs are used in various ways for different pedagogical purposes. For example, personal blogs are simply online journals that foster self-expression and self-reflection, whereas collective blogs involve an entire class or small groups of students who collaboratively construct L2 knowledge. Given that blogs are asynchronous CMC, authors write at their own pace without time pressure, which enables them to reflect critically upon the content. Network-based publishing also fosters learner autonomy, as students take charge of making their own decisions as to what and how much to include and when to publish their work (Lee 2010).

L2 research has shown that language learners benefit from using blogs. For example, reading blogs made by NS enhances an understanding of real-world communication and promotes cross-cultural awareness and skills (Lee 2009; Ware and Kramsch 2005). As for writing blogs, the study conducted by Liam Murray and Tríona Hourigan (2008) reveals that learners gain confidence in writing and develop their own approaches that suit their personal writing styles. Furthermore, students increase their motivation to write because they no longer just write for a sole instructor but rather for a broad audience (Lee 2009). In addition, blogs have been designed for cross-cultural exchange to promote global communication and intercultural awareness. For example, students gain cultural understanding from a variety of different perspectives by reading blogs written by NS (Ducate and Lomicka 2008). Another study by Idoia Elola and Ana Oskoz (2008) reports that the use of blogs enables study-abroad and at-home students to exchange cultural knowledge from personal perspectives and also to develop their intercultural competence. Similarly, in her recent CMC study, Lee (2012) found that blogging with NS afforded L2 learners the opportunity to gain cultural perspectives and raise their awareness of cross-cultural issues over the course of a semester study abroad program.

Tweeting

Twitter is a microblogging tool that enables users to exchange brief messages of up to 140 characters called tweets, including individual images and video links. Users create their accounts via the Twitter site (twitter.com) and use a computer or mobile device to connect, communicate, and collaborate with others through quick exchanges. In addition, the # symbol, called a hashtag, allows users to create communities of people interested in the same topic and to search for tweets that have a common topic as well. L2 educators have implemented social networking tools such as Twitter in their teaching. For example, instructors post homework and/or brief questions to which students respond. To build continuity, students are asked to follow their peers on Twitter to comment on their tweets. Tweeting appears to be less intimidating for shy students who may be reluctant to participate in face-to-face discussions. Among other advantages, Twitter builds learners' sense of classroom community, increases their engagement in language learning, and enhances their knowledge of the target culture by interacting with NS beyond traditional classroom boundaries (Antenos-Conforti 2009; Lomicka and Lord 2012).

Findings based on the limited research on the effectiveness of Twitter on L2 learning reveal that students were motivated to tweet their peers to share and exchange information about their lives and classes, as they found tweets relevant to how the target language is used in the target countries. Other researchers shared the similar view that L2 learners benefited from reading and posting tweets about happenings in their lives (Lomicka and Lord 2012). With regard to intercultural learning, Twitter has been used for L2 learners to chat about current and cultural events with NS outside of the classroom. As a result, tweeting not only fosters social presence and community building (Antenos-Conforti, 2009) but also enhances cross-cultural communication and understanding (Ullrich, Borau, and Stepanyan 2010). The limit of 140 characters, however, presents challenges to students when trying to communicate complex thoughts. Moreover, when using Twitter for intercultural exchange, students feel frustrated and discouraged by not being able to receive responses from their cross-cultural partners in a timely fashion (Lomicka and Lord, 2012). To this end, instructors play a crucial role in facilitating tweeting by guiding and monitoring students' progress and discussing problematic areas with students in face-to-face meetings.

Podcasting

Podcasting is delivering online audio content through an RSS (Really Simple Syndication) feed; listeners can then subscribe to their favorite podcasts. Podcasts can be downloaded automatically to a computer using media player applications, such as iTunes (apple.com/itunes). Podcasting is appealing and supports language acquisition because it allows learners to listen to authentic recordings on a personal computer as well as to record and publish their own talks. Anyone can easily create and publish their own voice recordings using freely available software, such as Audacity (audacity.sourceforge.net) and GarageBand (www.apple.com/ilife/garageband). Audio recordings are typically converted to MP3 files and uploaded to available hosting sites or publishing services, such as PodOmatic (podomatic.com) and Podbean (podbean.com).

Language learners often have limited opportunities to be exposed to authentic input (listening) and produce output (speaking) in a traditional classroom setting. Listening to NS broadcasts enhances the real-world use of interpretative aural skills. For listening practice, teachers can search for appropriate language podcasts and make them accessible to students. For instance, Notes in Spanish (notesinspanish.com) offers podcasts about real-life topics in Spanish conversations from beginning to advanced levels. Based on students' language proficiency, the instructor can assign students to listen to specific podcasts. Another approach to podcasting is to engage students in producing their own voice recordings, which are then exchanged as audio files with another class or students from other cultures (Lee 2009; Stanley 2006). According to Lee (2009), creating podcasts is less anxiety-provoking than speaking in front of a class. The process of recording podcasts not only enhances students' pronunciation, but also boosts their speaking ability. Research shows that podcasts facilitate the development of learners' listening and speaking skills, including their pronunciation (Ducate and Lomicka 2009; McCarty, 2005; Rosell-Aguilar 2007).

Online Intercultural Exchange Project

Based on the previous discussion of Web 2.0 technologies for L2 instruction including intercultural learning, this section describes an intercultural exchange project between Spanish and American university students and demonstrates the importance of integrating sound pedagogical design of tasks in conjunction with blogs and podcasting for the development of learners' different cultural perspectives. As Lee (2005) points out, teachers need to take into account effective pedagogical principles, including specific instructional goals and procedures as well as technological tools, at the stage of implementation of web technologies in order to ensure optimal learning outcomes. This section will provide a detailed description of the current project in three parts: first, the project setting and the students who participated in the project; second, the objectives and structure of the project in conjunction with Web 2.0 tools and task-based activities; and third, the outcomes of the project, focusing on both general and specific students' observations along with pedagogical implications.

Setting of the Project

The researcher carried out the project over the course of one semester. One advanced English class from the University of León in Spain and one advanced Spanish class from the University of New Hampshire in the United States participated in the exchange. The participants from both groups ranged between 20 and 26 years of age. In general, students do not have the opportunity to use the target language to interact with NS outside of class, as they live in small towns and cities where the native language is the only language used for daily communication. To provide students with increased opportunities for authentic language practice and cross-cultural communication, they participated in a Spanish-American intercultural exchange. The researcher and the partner teacher worked together to design the project and task-based activities, which were part of course assignments (see "Structure of the Project" later in this chapter for more details).

To facilitate the online exchange, the researcher implemented several Web 2.0 tools in the project. All participants used Twitter to send and receive tweets throughout the exchange. Both groups used Blogger to create personal and group blogs using a Google account. To make podcasts, students used Audioboo (audioboo.fm), an application that enables users to share sound files. In addition, some students used iMovie (Mac) and Movie Maker (PC) for video recordings. Despite the fact that both groups were comfortable with Web 2.0 technology, including browsing information online, email, and text chat, none of them had used Twitter, blogs, or podcasts for L2 learning prior to the project. Most students were tech-savvy and comfortable using social media (e.g., Facebook) and mobile devices (e.g., iPod, iPhone). Thus, no training on how to use Web 2.0 tools was required. The instructors encouraged students to use tutorial videos and online help sites for assistance (e.g., help.blogger.com for Blogger).

Objectives of the Project

To offer additional support for exploring L2 and the target culture, the project set three main objectives: (1) to build students' intercultural competence through the use of Web 2.0 tools; (2) to create a collaborative learning community where the students co-construct meaning and form with their peers using task-based activities; and (3) to foster linguistic awareness through peer feedback as part of an online exchange.

Structure of the Project

As part of the course requirement, the students completed three major consecutive tasks (Table 4.1) outside of class, which were worth 30 percent of their final grade. Tasks were scheduled in the course syllabus, and each task took 3 to 4 weeks to complete.

The Intercultural Exchange Project consisted of three stages, described here.

Stage 1: Getting to know each other via Twitter. According to Lee (2007), it is essential to provide students with opportunities for building interpersonal relationships in order to reduce discomfort levels and emotional tensions. Students used Twitter as a social media tool to establish good rapport and build group dynamics. At the beginning of the exchange, students set up Twitter accounts and followed the instructor on Twitter. Students then sent tweets to introduce themselves to their distant partners. To facilitate conversations around specific topics, hashtags (e.g., *#Leónblog*) were used to allow those who were interested in the same topic to follow easily. Both groups spent 2 weeks tweeting each other to share and exchange personal interests, academic work, and cultural events. In addition, the instructor tweeted students with updates on coursework and the exchange project. Students also used Twitter to discuss course assignments, brainstorm ideas, and make decisions on the topics of their blogs and podcasts.

Stage 2: Exchanging cultural perspectives via blogging. The U.S. students created individual blogs, whereas the students from Spain were divided into groups of two or three to produce collaborative blogs. Each blog consisted of a minimum of five entries (see Table 4.1). Although the instructors did not participate in any blogs, they were available to answer questions and offer assistance. Upon the completion of blog assignments, all URLs were posted and made available in the class wiki for viewing. Students read and critiqued their partners' blogs. One of

Table 4.1 Topics and Tasks for Intercultural Exchange Project

Topics	Tasks
Blogs: A Taste of Local Culture and People	You are required to produce a blog concerning university student lives, your hometown, and the Spanish/American culture. Your blog should contain a minimum of five entries. You should also use external links, photos, audio, and videos to support the content of each entry. Upon the completion of the assignment, blogs will be posted in the Moodle class wiki to invite your NS partners to make comments on the content as well as provide linguistic feedback.
Podcasts: Controversial Issues	For this task, you will work with your classmate to produce podcasts concerning controversial topics. Each pair should choose a different topic. You will explain the current situation in the United States/Spain. You will debate the issue, discuss different arguments, and conclude the discussion by asking your Spanish partners for their reactions. Your recording should last a minimum of 5 minutes and should be embedded into your blog.
Peer Feedback: Content and Language	You are required to make comments on your NS partners' blogs and podcasts. In addition, you should provide linguistic feedback by addressing their vocabulary and grammar errors. You may use L1 or L2 to write comments in their blogs.

the major benefits of using asynchronous CMC is the opportunity to focus on form (Lee 2008). Thus, students provided corrective feedback to foster linguistic awareness. The instructor did not give any specific instructions to the students. They made their own choices regarding how much feedback should be provided to their native speaker partners.

Stage 3: Discussing controversial issues via podcasting. After creating their blog entries, students recorded podcasts dealing with controversial topics, such as abortion and gay marriage. Students worked in pairs to make podcasts for their native speaker partners. Each recording was made within a dialogue format, in which two students discussed and debated the chosen topic. The instructor assisted students in finding supportive resources for controversial issues. Students wrote, rehearsed, and finally recorded the script using their own computers. In addition, they incorporated musical interludes into their recordings. Each recording lasted approximately 5 to 6 minutes. The recordings were embedded into students' blogs for viewing and commenting. The instructor did not assign any particular podcasts to specific individuals. Students were free to listen to any recordings that interested them and made comments on each others' blogs.

Outcomes of the Project

Students' Observations of the Intercultural Exchange

Although the short period of time using each tool would not directly result in improvement of language skills and the development of learners' intercultural awareness, students' online survey feedback was extremely positive (Table 4.2).

Table 4.2   Student Reactions to Web Tools and Online Exchanges

Statements of the Survey	Mean	SD
1. I enjoyed creating blogs/podcasts for the exchange project.	4.25	0.45
2. I liked how we used Twitter to interact with each other.	3.86	0.51
3. Creating blogs and podcasts was beneficial to me.	4.58	0.52
4. Reading blog entries and listening to podcasts enhanced my understanding of the target culture.	4.42	0.67
5. Cultural topics were interesting and informative.	4.33	0.65
6. Making podcasts was fun and useful for me.	4.08	0.29
7. I found online tasks time-consuming.	3.92	0.66
8. I found peer feedback and error corrections useful.	4.25	0.62
9. I was comfortable providing feedback to my peers.	3.08	0.67
10. Overall, it was a positive experience for me.	4.33	0.65

Overall, students were satisfied with many aspects of the project (statement 10). The experience with Web 2.0 transformed the way that students viewed intercultural learning. Neither group had difficulty accessing blogs and podcasts online. In Spain, broadband service offered by Telefónica S.A. provides a high-speed internet connection. Thus, most students from León had reliable internet access at home or school, and some of them used a mobile device to connect with their cross-cultural partners. The following excerpts drawn from the online surveys exhibit how the students reflected on the effectiveness of Web 2.0 tools:

> I believe a social media tool like Twitter can be used to create stronger relationships among my peers. ... This type of immediacy and prevalence helps me interact with my Spanish partners in an interesting and enjoyable way.

It was an eye-opening experience for me. Through tweeting and blogging, I learned so much about young people and their lives in the northern province of the region Castilla in Spain. It was really a great way to get to know one's home culture through online exchange with native speakers.

While more than 50 percent of the students enjoyed using Twitter (statement 2), some students were reluctant to engage in social media for academic purposes. One student, for example, remarked:

I would do it because I was asked to do so. I do not think it is inevitable using Twitter academically. In fact I hope it is not, because I find technology to be overwhelming as it is. I already stare at a screen for too many hours per day.

Clearly, the student did not find social networking necessary for her academic work. To make the intercultural exchange more compelling, teachers should make students aware of not just the use of social media itself, but of the potentially significant impact that social networking has on intercultural dialogue with NS across geographical boundaries.

With respect to blogs and podcasts, the majority of the students noted that they enjoyed creating them for their NS partners (statement 1). Many students also acknowledged that they benefited from reading and commenting on others' (statement 3). The following excerpts drawn from online postings (translated to English) further demonstrate how much students enjoyed the exchange with the Spanish partners and learned about the traditions and customs of Spain:

I enjoyed the blog. I love all the pictures and the descriptions of the local food in León. The nightlife seems really fun, and it really is a great idea to serve tapas with each drink.

This is an awesome post. These festivals seem so fun! Have you guys been to all of them? La Tomatina seems outrageous, but like it would be a blast! Have any of you participated? You must just get completely covered in tomatoes—LOL. Las Fallas is probably really amazing.

Students further pointed out that topics were revealing and informative (statement 5) and that they would not have gained such a deep understanding of certain aspects of the target culture had they not had the opportunity to interact with the students from Spain (statement 4). For example, one student wrote the following comment on the survey:

> I learned a lot about Spanish culture that I didn't know, particularly some of the less mainstream music and some festivals that I wasn't aware of. It was great to get some of that information, because it's not necessarily something you get in a classroom.

These findings prove that learning the target culture from NS' experiences and perspectives is more meaningful than the surface learning of a set of simple facts about the target culture in a traditional classroom setting, as shown in the previous research (Hauck and Youngs 2008; Ware and Kramsch 2005). Similar to the findings reported in Lee's (2009) asynchronous CMC research, students observed that they felt a sense of pride and ownership, as they invested a great deal of time and energy into creating blogs and podcasts. Furthermore, they highlighted that Web 2.0 had made it possible for them to connect with their cross-cultural partners and gain different cultural perspectives from them.

As for podcasts, students appreciated the opportunity to make podcasts for their distant partners and found it appealing and beneficial to them (statement 6). Among other advantages, students found listening to their own recordings very helpful, as they learned how to make improvements in their speaking. Moreover, hearing their Spanish partners' responses to their voice recordings made clearer the linguistic gap between native and non-native speakers of Spanish, including the pronunciation. These findings are in line with those from other studies (Ducate and Lomicka 2009; Rosell-Aguilar 2007). When asking students to comment on their partners' podcasts, they made positive remarks, as shown in the following excerpts from blog postings:

> Very interesting podcasts! It's good to see that there is a lot of discussion about these issues throughout the whole world. Right now abortion is legal throughout the U.S., but it is a constant issue up for debate, and many states have imposed

different guidelines to make getting an abortion more difficult. It all comes down to definitions here. Will pregnancy "threaten" the "health" of the mother? Is it considered "partial-birth abortion"? There are still lots of questions and a ton of debate about the issue, and it changes from state to state!

Your second podcast was really informative! I hadn't heard of many of those word double meanings before. *Coger* is always the one that we joke about. We have a professor that always asks if we are going to *coger* the bus, and we always have to respond to him: "Well, we are going to *tomar,* not *coger* it.

These examples clearly demonstrate that podcasting affords L2 learners an effective way of discussing controversial and linguistic (e.g., lexical variation) issues in an internet-mediated social environment. In particular, interacting with their distant partners through voice recordings not only connected students in a way that written text cannot, but also built their confidence in using the target language for real-world communication.

Clearly, students enhanced their advanced computer skills by making podcasts. They, however, found the task time-consuming (statement 7). For example, one student made the following comment:

I was glad to use Audioboo to make two podcasts with my classmate. It was fun. However, I must say that it took us a lot of time to make them. We had to record them several times before embedding them to the blog.

Another challenge was finding a common time to work with the classmates, and some students felt rushed to complete their assignments to meet the deadlines. Strategies for voice recordings need to be addressed before students execute the assignments. It would be helpful to provide students with good sample podcasts and further discuss with them how to go about creating high-quality recordings (Lee 2009). Another suggestion is to encourage students to write up an outline with a list of items to keep them on track so they don't lose their place in the middle of recording.

Linguistic Feedback and Strategies Used by Both Groups

As part of the online exchange, both groups provided feedback to each other to address linguistic problems. Overwhelmingly, more than 80 percent of the students were in favor of peer feedback on linguistic form and found it helpful to them (statement 8). The following quotation drawn from online surveys illustrates that the student found linguistic feedback valuable:

> I enjoyed most receiving the linguistic feedback from our peers in León. They were able to provide feedback on subtle errors that I commit frequently.

The findings corroborate those found in a study conducted by Robert O'Dowd and Paige Ware (2008), which stressed that students preferred an inclusion of peer feedback on linguistic form as part of the online exchange and found it useful for the development of their interlanguage. Another striking finding is that nearly 40 percent of the students did not feel comfortable addressing linguistic errors made by their partners (statement 9). One student commented that error correction via the Comment feature of Blogger was not a good format for linguistic feedback because the overall theme of the course content focused on intercultural learning. The same student also admitted that she was reluctant to make error correction in an open forum because she did not want to embarrass the Spanish partners. Another student pointed out that it was challenging to explain complex grammar points with clarity through writing and further suggested using audio recordings to provide oral feedback, especially regarding error correction on pronunciation.

Blog comments show that both groups tended to use English to provide linguistic feedback on inappropriate lexical and syntactical items. They were inclined to address the inaccurate or inappropriate use of grammar points. The following excerpts from online postings exemplify grammar feedback given by both American and Spanish students:

- I could barely find any errors in this blog. One little thing I found is when you say "role in the Spanish literature." You don't need "the"; just "role in Spanish literature" is correct.

- I would rephrase your sentence "Those who doesn't study it hard" to "Those who don't study it a lot."

- *"Hasta que hayan los recursos"* [should be] *"Hasta que haya recursos."* (The verb should be singular.)

- [Instead of] *"No pueden practicar,"* *"No pueden entrenar"* is a better option.

One common feedback strategy seen in both groups was the use of positive comments on the quality of their partners' linguistic skills. Words of approval, such as *excellent, impressive,* and *awesome,* appeared repeatedly during the feedback process. For example, the students complimented the high quality of their partners' linguistic skills in the following examples:

> Your English is EXCELLENT. I could barely find any errors, and the ones I did notice I really had to look for. Instead of "lasted the years," I would say "lasted the test of time."

> By the way, you speak Spanish better than me, and that's great. Normally, when we talk about the author of a novel, we say *"de"* (*un libro de J. Safran*) instead of *"por"* (*un libro escrito por J. Safran*). But they are insignificant mistakes. Congrats for your Spanish and for this entry.

Pragmatically competent speakers know how to express themselves appropriately in a social context. These excerpts clearly demonstrate that the advanced speakers were aware of using compliments to diminish intimidation before commenting on their partners' linguistic problems. The result coincides with the findings found in the recent study conducted by Lee (2011), who found that L2 learners used effective pragmatic strategies (e.g., compliments, requests) during computer-mediated social interactions.

Pedagogical Implications and Conclusion

Web 2.0 technologies have opened new doors for language learning and teaching. The development of learners' intercultural competence should be the core of L2 instruction in the age of globalization (Thorne 2003). Despite some challenges, the project demonstrates how students used social networking tools for intercultural exchange in ways that were pedagogically effective. Online task-based learning was meaningful and stimulating, as students were actively involved in the learning process through interaction and collaboration. Several practical pedagogical issues need to be taken into account when implementing Web 2.0 tools in future online projects. First, blogging should evolve over a longer time span, with more time allocated to each assignment in order to develop a long-term effect on L2 writing. Second, voice recordings using readily available software should be used on a regular basis to build oral fluency. For example, VoiceThread (voicethread.com), a website that allows users to share and comment on content via voice, is particularly effective for speaking practice. Third, the combined use of Web 2.0 tools and task-based instruction proved to be effective in empowering students' intercultural communication. Instructors should integrate topics relevant to students' interests and debatable world issues into network-based instruction. Fourth, L2 learners should use synchronous CMC, such as voice and video chat via Skype (skype.com), to increase real-time online interaction. Finally, linguistic feedback constitutes learning. It is essential for instructors to create appropriate awareness-raising activities through which focus on form is guaranteed while meaning-oriented interaction is shared during the CMC.

In closing, digital technology and social networking are appealing to today's learners. Tweeting, blogging, and podcasting in the target language offer promising benefits for L2 learners, as they interact and collaborate with NS within a socially bounded learning environment. Only through authentic contexts and natural discourse does classroom-learned language become meaningful for real-world communication. Through online cross-cultural dialogue, students become globally conscious and competent. While new technologies continue to emerge and impact L2 instruction, a task-based approach to language learning and intercultural interaction along with sound pedagogical principles clearly takes on an essential role in its effective use. It is hoped that this project has provided new insight into the practicality of implementing Web 2.0 tools in the development of learners' language skills and intercultural competence.

References

Antenos-Conforti, Enza. 2009. "Microblogging on Twitter: Social Networking in Intermediate Italian Classes." In *The Next Generation: Social Networking and Online Collaboration in Foreign Language Learning*, edited by Lara Lomicka and

Gillian Lord, 59–90. San Marcos, TX: Computer Assisted Language Instruction Consortium.

Belz, Julie. 2003. "Linguistic Perspectives on the Development of Intercultural Competence in Telecollaboration." *Language Learning & Technology* 7(2): 68–117.

Belz, Julie, and Steve Thorne, eds. 2006. *Internet-Mediated Intercultural Foreign Language Education.* Boston: Heinle & Heinle.

Byram, Michael. 1997. *Teaching and Assessing Intercultural Communicative Competence.* Clevedon, UK: Multilingual Matters.

Carney, Nat. 2009. "Blogging in Foreign Language Education." In *Handbook of Research on Web 2.0 and Second Language Learning,* edited by Michael Thomas, 292–312. Hershey, PA: IGI Global.

Ducate, Lara C., and Lara L. Lomicka. 2008. "Adventures in the Blogosphere: From Blog Readers to Blog Writers." *Computer Assisted Language Learning* 21(1): 9–28. oostburgteam.pbworks.com/f/adventures+in+blogging.pdf.

———. 2009. "Podcasting: An Effective Tool for Honing Language Students' Pronunciation?" *Language Learning & Technology* 13(3): 66–86. llt.msu.edu/vol13 num3/ducatelomicka.pdf.

Elola, Idoia, and Ana Oskoz. 2008. "Blogging: Fostering Intercultural Competence Development in Foreign Language and Study Abroad Contexts." *Foreign Language Annals* 41(3): 454–478.

Guth, Sarah, and Francesca Helm, eds. 2010. *Telecollaboration 2.0: Language, Literacies, and Intercultural Learning in the 21st Century.* Bern: Peter Lang.

Hauck, Mirjam. 2007. "Critical Success Factors in a TRIDEM Exchange." *ReCALL* 19(2): 202–223.

Hauck, Mirjam, and Bonnie L. Youngs. 2008. "Telecollaboration in Multimodal Environments: The Impact on Task Design and Learner Interaction." *Computer Assisted Language Learning* 21(2): 87–124.

Jin, Li, and Tony Erben. 2007. "Intercultural Learning via Instant Messenger Interaction." *CALICO Journal* 24(2): 291–311.

Kinginger, Celeste, and Julie Belz. 2005. "Sociocultural Perspectives on Pragmatic Development in Foreign Language Learning: Case Studies from Telecollaboration and Study Abroad." *Intercultural Pragmatics* 2(4): 369–421.

Lee, Lina. 2004. "Learners' Perspectives on Networked Collaborative Interaction with Native Speakers of Spanish in the U.S." *Language Learning & Technology* 8(1): 83–100. llt.msu.edu/vol8num1/lee/default.html.

———. 2005. "Using Web-Based Instruction to Promote Active Learning: Learners' Perspectives." *CALICO Journal* 23(1): 139–156.

———. 2008. "Focus-on-Form Through Collaborative Scaffolding in Expert-to-Novice Online Interaction." *Language Learning & Technology* 12(3): 53–72. llt. msu.edu/vol12num3/lee.pdf.

———. 2009. "Promoting Intercultural Exchanges With Blogs and Podcasting: A Study of Spanish-American Telecollaboration." *Computer Assisted Language Learning* 22(5): 425–443.

———. 2010. "Fostering Reflective Writing and Interactive Exchange Through Blogging in an Advanced Language Course." *ReCALL* 22(2): 212–227.

———. 2011. "Focus-on-Form Through Peer Feedback in a Spanish-American Telecollaborative Exchange." *Language Awareness* 20(4): 343–357.

———. 2012. "Engaging Study Abroad Students in Intercultural Learning through Blogging and Ethnographic Interviews." *Foreign Language Annals* 45(1): 7–21.

Levy, Mike, and Glenn Stockwell. 2006. *CALL Dimensions: Options and Issues in Computer-Assisted Language Learning.* Mahwah, NJ: Lawrence Erlbaum.

Lomicka, Lara, and Gillian Lord. 2012. "A Tale of Tweets: Analyzing Microblogging Among Language Learners." *System* 40(1): 48–63.

McCarty, Steve. 2005. "Spoken Internet to Go: Popularization Through Podcasting." *JALT CALL Journal* 1(2): 67–74.

Miguela, Antonia D. 2007. "Models of Telecollaboration (3): eTwinning." In *Online Intercultural Exchange: An Introduction for Foreign Language Teachers,* edited by Robert O'Dowd, 85–106. Clevedon, UK: Multilingual Matters.

Murray, Liam, and Tríona Hourigan. 2008. "Blogs for Specific Purposes: Expressivist or Socio-cognitivist Approach?" *ReCALL* 20(1): 82–97. www.postgradolinguistica. ucv.cl/dev/documentos/90,969,7%20Blogs_murray_2008.pdf.

O'Dowd, Robert, ed. 2007. *Online Intercultural Exchange: An Introduction for Foreign Language Teachers.* Clevedon, UK: Multilingual Matters.

O'Dowd, Robert, and Markus Ritter. 2006. "Understanding and Working With 'Failed Communication' in Telecollaborative Exchanges." *CALICO Journal* 23(2): 623–642.

O'Dowd, Robert, and Paige D. Ware. 2008. "Peer Feedback on Language Form in Telecollaboration." *Language Learning & Technology* 12(1): 43–63. llt.msu.edu/ vol12num1/pdf/wareodowd/default.html.

Pinkman, Kathleen. 2005. "Using Blogs in the Foreign Language Classroom: Encouraging Learner Independence." *JALT CALL Journal* 1(1): 12–24.

Richardson, Will. 2010. *Blogs, Wikis, Podcasts, and Other Powerful Web Tools for Classrooms,* 2nd ed. Thousand Oaks, CA: Corwin Press.

Rosell-Aguilar, Fernando. 2007. "Top of the Pods: In Search of a Podcasting 'Podagogy' for Language Learning." *Computer Assisted Language Learning* 20(5): 471–492.

Sauro, Shannon. 2009. "Computer-Mediated Corrective Feedback and the Development of L2 Grammar." *Language Learning & Technology* 13(1): 96–120. llt.msu.edu/ vol13num1/sauro.pdf.

Stanley, Graham. 2006. "Podcasting: Audio on the Internet Comes of Age." *TESL-EJ* 9(4): 1–7. tesl-ej.org/ej36/int.html.

Thorne, Steve. 2003. "Artifacts and Cultures-of-Use in Intercultural Communication." *Language Learning & Technology* 7(2): 38–67. llt.msu.edu/vol7num2/thorne/default.html.

Ullrich, Carsten, Kerstin Borau, and Karen Stepanyan. 2010. "Who Students Interact With? A Social Network Analysis Perspective on the Use of Twitter in Language Learning." *Sustaining TEL: From Innovation to Learning and Practice. Lecture Notes in Computer Science* 6383: 432–437. www.carstenullrich.net/pubs/Ullrich10Who.pdf.

Ware, Paige D., and Claire Kramsch. 2005. "Toward an Intercultural Stance: Teaching German and English Through Telecollaboration." *Modern Language Journal* 89(2): 190–205.

CHAPTER 5

The iPad as a Tool for Global Education: Opportunities and Limitations

Kathryn Mendez

With today's technological advances, it is difficult to imagine education in developed nations without the aid of computers, interactive white-boards, and online textbooks. Teachers of all subjects are being brought into the profession understanding that part of their responsibility to their students is to understand and integrate some sort of technology into their lesson plans; without it, many people feel that students would be at a disadvantage, since they, too, will eventually be entering a work force where technology is inevitable and rapidly changing. Ironically, by the time this article is written, the technology of today will be outdated, and, therefore the specifics in this piece must be seen as constantly in a state of flux. While the examples of technology discussed here will have evolved, technology will most likely still have a significant presence in the classroom and should continue to be assessed and discussed by those who teach and advocate for global awareness.

Since it would be nearly impossible to write a concise piece on the number of existing technological resources available to enhance global awareness and facilitate the connection between students in developed nations with their peers in developing nations, these pages will focus specifically on the iPad as a possible tool to help students and educators achieve this goal. In this chapter, the iPad serves as the focus of the study, but it is just one of the many possible tablet technologies available to students. Other tablets with similar technologies are the Intel Atom and the Samsung Galaxy Note, for example. Many of the suggestions in this article could be applied to other types of tablets, although the iPad has several applications that are specific to its use. Many schools in the United States are experimenting with making the switch from textbooks and notebooks to iPads. This is happening at all levels, from pre-kindergarten to colleges and universities. Recently, for example, I observed a kindergarten classroom that had iPads available for students to explore at a certain time each day. They were surrounded by a type of soft, protective bumper meant to help lower the effects of wear and tear on the machines by young users. In kindergarten, each student was not expected to have an iPad; however, in the same institution, the middle school and high school levels were in the process of phasing out textbooks and introducing iPads as a school-wide requirement. In this way, it is expected that students will be able to keep all of their textbooks, notes, and graded assignments in one small convenient place that has applications designed for enhanced organization and availability of resources literally at a student's fingertips.

While some might shudder at the idea of condensing traditional classroom materials into one machine weighing less than two pounds, others are excited at this prospect and have embraced it with energy and curiosity. This kind of mixed reaction to the iPad in the classroom was evident in my own research at an independent secondary school. While working with a grant that allowed high school-level teachers to borrow an iPad for educational use over the course of a semester, I was able to talk to colleagues in my own department as well as attend seminars and visit similar schools where the same kind of research was in process. Those who presented at the seminars were very enthusiastic about the capabilities for the iPad, while, at the same time, not everyone volunteered immediately to borrow and research the machines. Even as a technology enthusiast, I struggled somewhat when researching the iPad, particularly when observing at other schools and seminars, because it was somewhat difficult to achieve an online connection in order to participate in group iPad activities. The question is whether it is worth continuing with the iPad and taking the time to troubleshoot such issues, or if those issues are offset by the user-friendly appeal of the iPad. From personal experience, I would say that any institution trying the iPads should prepare for a mixed response to the change from both students and faculty.

Regardless of whether one embraces educational technology, it makes sense when looking at the global picture to ask how the introduction of devices such as the iPad will be useful in helping connect students and educators in different parts of the world once the newness and excitement of these devices wears off. Just a few centuries ago, books were only for a privileged few in the way that iPads are today. Books were expensive, and most traditional classrooms did not have any, let alone one for each student. As print became more accessible, it became the norm for many communities to have individual book collections and public libraries, while in other parts of the world today, books are still not as readily available in classrooms and households. Their cost and upkeep continue to be prohibitive for some, and their existence continues to be linked to socioeconomic and political issues such as economic power, intellectual freedom, and censorship. It is worth considering the following questions: What information does the book contain? How does censorship play into its availability? Who is in charge of deciding which books contain quality material? What are the consequences for those who disagree with those in charge? In what ways does ownership of certain books put a person in political or social danger? These are just a few of the many questions linked to book ownership on a global level. By looking not only at the history but also at the current reality of books, it is possible to learn a few things about what might happen with the iPad as an educational tool in a similar context.

This is not to say, however, that the iPad experience will be the same as the one with a printed text. On the contrary, the iPad offers many possibilities that traditional books do not. One concrete example of how technology has had a significant impact on intellectual power and global change is in the case of the Arab Spring, which began in 2010. Felipe Campante and Davin Chor (2012) have noted in their work that there is a direct connection between education and participation in political activity; it would make sense that the role of technology in education would play a part in the way such activity is shared with the world. It has also been noted that increased technological resources and familiarity with social media played an essential role in helping political protesters organize demonstrations and communicate with each other (Kassim 2012). In addition, Campante and Chor (2012) note that "the Arab world indeed witnessed both substantial investment in education and poor labor market conditions, [so] it is plausible to think that this combination was important as a root cause of the Arab Spring" (179).

Moving beyond the Arab world and on to a larger global perspective, another major difference between the iPad and books is that the iPad can offer infinitely changing content. This is incredibly important for those with limited economic resources in communities at all stages of economic development. iPad users have access to countless sources of information via the internet, and they also, in many cases, have the ability to download the most recent edition of books for a fraction of the cost that they would pay to purchase a hard copy of a newly revised edition of a text. In the case of textbooks, this is particularly important. Textbook companies must regularly revise the editions of their textbooks, resulting in great expense and waste for those who use their products and wish to have the most recent editions (Pressler 2004). With online textbooks, these updates can be made regularly and be more accessible and less expensive to obtain for students and educational institutions, although, unfortunately, the cost of purchasing a license to use an interactive electronic textbook website is quickly catching up to the cost of purchasing new editions of textbooks. This only adds to the problematic dynamic that makes a variety of educational options available only to a small percentage of global citizens who have the economic power to purchase them.

In the developing world, the cost of purchasing and maintaining technology such as the iPad is just as problematic as the prohibitive cost of books: A student who wants access to an electronic textbook must first secure access to the internet and then be able to purchase a license for the textbook online; in many cases, this license needs to be renewed annually. If an educational institution desires to assist students in gaining access to online resources, the institution also must put forth the necessary economic resources to do so. Funding for internet access and maintenance, training for educators, and the ability to purchase portable electronic devices such as iPads for students still present a significant barrier not only in developing nations but in all nations, with the exception of the most privileged communities within them. Here one can see a cyclical imbalance, since those who possess a high level of comfort with technological devices are often the most desirable candidates in the work force, yet only those with the economic means to purchase technology or who live in an area where their schools can afford to do so can access this knowledge and therefore have a greater chance to find employment that pays a living wage. There is a great deal of literature available that discusses the idea of the "digital divide" both inside of individual nations and on a global scale (for example, Pippa Norris [2001] explores the topic in great detail).

It is necessary to look at how the global digital divide can be bridged in order to introduce iPad technology into areas of the world where there has not traditionally been significant infrastructural or personal economic support for updated technology in education. Phillip Ein-Dor, Michael Myers, and K.S. Raman (1997) discuss the importance of national culture as an indicator of whether education can be supported by technological supplements such as iPads. They state that while countries may vary "in terms of underlying cultural factors [such as] ethnicity, language, and religion ... they [the countries that have had much success with introducing technology into their markets and industries] are remarkably similar in terms of indicators of general level of development [in terms of] life expectancy, infant mortality, literacy, and newspaper circulation" (73). The three countries discussed in the article by Ein-Dor, Myers, and Raman are Israel, Singapore, and New Zealand. If one were to follow the model of thought presented by this theory, it would appear that countries that are not as developed as these three nations and that do not have such similar traits in their national culture may not be able to support the necessary requirements to include iPad technology in their classrooms. After all, iPads are impractical unless their users have had at least some basic training in how to manipulate their applications and protect them from damage and loss.

While the argument regarding national culture is quite strong both in theory and practice, it does not mean that countries that do not share the same national culture as developed nations are doomed to fail at introducing technology into their educational curriculum. It simply means that they might need some support from outside communities to help them begin the process of adapting some parts of their national culture while at the same time maintaining respect for traditional values and norms within each community. A number of communities might not feel that the iPad is necessary for a valuable education, and if that is the case, such a decision should be respected by even the most well-intentioned educators. After all, national culture is a fluid and flexible idea; it can be a source of conflict and frustration, but it can also be fertile ground for experimentation and change if there are enough individuals (both from within and outside) devoted to instilling positive and voluntary changes, whatever those changes may be.

Observing language teachers in the U.S. has shed light on how the iPad can be used to break down linguistic barriers and thereby allow students in developed countries to communicate with and better understand the realities of their counterparts throughout the world. One of the first and most basic functions that an iPad can serve in the language classroom is that of making tools for self-study and practice more immediately accessible to language students. A most significant complaint about language acquisition in the current system in the U.S. is that over weekends and school vacations, progress in the language classroom is lost because students do not use their skills and therefore forget newly learned verb forms and vocabulary. With a tool such as the iPad, students not only have the possibility of installing language acquisition programs (such as Rosetta Stone software), but they also have access to dictionaries, online translators, and flashcard applications on a portable device on which they could study for a few minutes while waiting at a bus stop or in a doctor's office.

Applications such as Evernote (evernote.com) and Google Docs (docs.google.com) support the idea of team curriculum among educators and communication among classmates both during school hours and when the students are outside of class. These types of applications, though not designed specifically for language acquisition, allow students to do group work (for example, collaborating on a document) even when they cannot be physically together, while still being observed by their teacher, who has control over the class functions and toolbar options. Nearpod (nearpod.com) is yet another application for the iPad, where students can work on presentations that can include videos, drawings, slide shows, and text (Figure 5.1); teachers may also quiz their students on course content through the same application or show sample presentations when introducing the project. Students have the ability to browse both the internet and other Nearpod slides to assist them in forming their own projects.

These applications also have relatively secure options that allow a student to turn in a quiz or project to the teacher without having the ability to go back and change it or to access the work of other students without authorization.

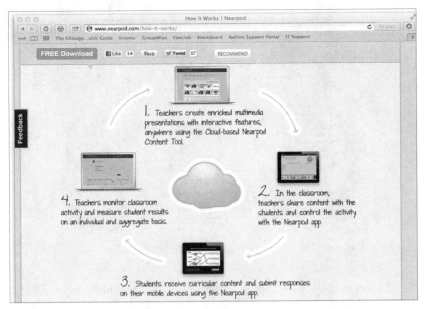

Figure 5.1   The features of Nearpod

While Evernote, Google Docs, and Nearpod can be used for a wide range of subjects, there are other applications that hone in on specific aspects of language acquisition, such as grammar and vocabulary. Quizlet (quizlet.com), for example, has its own application for the iPad, and teachers can create their own quizzes that are then converted into games, flashcards, and quizzes for their students to study (Figure 5.2).

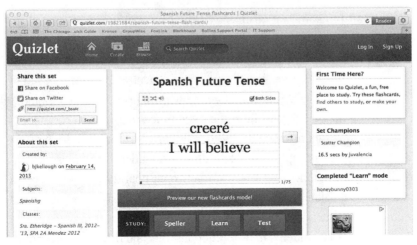

Figure 5.2   Quizlet

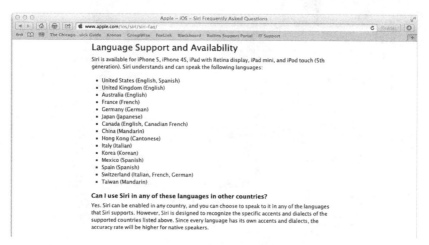

Figure 5.3   List of languages available on Siri

Screenchomp (itunes.apple.com/us/app/screenchomp/id442415881? mt=8) is similar to Quizlet in that it allows teachers and students a password-protected way to create and utilize language study tools pertinent to their particular class. The Siri application and iPad keyboard can also be configured to different languages (Figure 5.3), allowing language students to practice everyday routines in a language different from their native tongue.

Unlike reading textbooks, this process more closely resembles how human beings learn their first language: by practice and repetition of daily activities. Those with iPads also have access to FaceTime on their tablet, a video call program that enables a "virtual pen pal" relationship, which could be used to speak with someone from another country and develop relationships with people who speak their target language but are thousands of miles away and otherwise inaccessible. The Encuentros program, based in Morelos, Mexico, is a Spanish language-learning program that includes FaceTime with a teacher while at the same time utilizing chat room technology and internet referencing abilities (Figure 5.4). This program offers both private and group classes that allow the students to choose a convenient time to work from home in their own country and have access to a native speaker instructor to whom they can speak, type, and read uploaded documents and internet sources all in the target language. The result here is that students in different countries and different time zones who perhaps cannot travel abroad have access to interaction with other

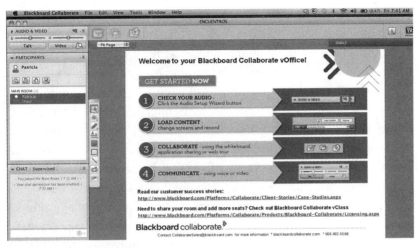

Figure 5.4   Encuentros program via Blackboard

students and language teachers who can provide feedback, assessments, lesson plans, and practice for an hourly fee.

It is also possible that students who choose to travel to countries of their target language can bring along a portable device such as an iPad and use it to orient themselves and communicate with fewer barriers. It is important to consider, however, the logistics of these suggestions. First, even in a wealthy country such as the U.S., only a privileged few would have access to a device such as an iPad. The average youth in the U.S. today cannot afford such a device. There are more inexpensive alternatives on the market, but they do not offer some of the applications, including Siri. Also, language acquisition programs, such as Rosetta Stone, are extremely cost-prohibitive and require a large investment of time and money that may not deliver results quickly enough to satisfy a language student. Furthermore, even if most young people in developed countries could afford an iPad, it does not guarantee that they could find or have access to peer counterparts in their target languages from developing countries due to the prohibitive cost of the technology and wireless internet access on both ends. Wireless access both in the U.S. and elsewhere has many limits. Many places all over the globe simply have no internet access, or if they do, its use may incur large expenses to data plans and is not accessible to the average citizen. It is also a very idealistic argument that all students in the U.S. or elsewhere would have unbridled access to technology for language acquisition and that they would use it independently in their free time outside of the language classroom. This being said, however, a true educator might respond to these challenges by insisting that education itself is based on curiosity, idealism, and the constant struggle to overcome these obstacles.

For school systems that have tried to integrate personal devices such as the iPad into their educational curricula, there have been mixed results. Studies from Australia, Canada, and the U.S. have all noted the need for a stable infrastructure to manage the integration of the iPad into everyday student work. Susan Crichton, Karen Pegler, and Duncan White concluded that a kind of technology task force must be assembled "to support the meaningful adoption and integration of educational technologies in the classroom. This team works with IT support staff, teachers, and partners from industry and the university to integrate innovative practice with both theory and classroom realities" (2012, 24). The contrast between theory and reality is the basis for many of the arguments around iPad technologies in an educational setting. Are students—particularly older students with already established notions of study skills—psychologically willing to accept a new technique into their daily routines if these routines were already successful for them before the arrival of the new technology? Are school systems prepared to support faculty and staff in continual training that keeps up with the pace of software updates and hardware configurations? Certainly these questions were asked when it was first suggested that computer labs be introduced into schools, followed later by laptop technology and institution-wide email communication. While the laptop itself is now becoming almost a standard of the professional world in nations at all stages of development, in the field of education it is a particularly exciting challenge to draw in personal devices such as the iPad because of their interactive features such as touch technology. While Mehryar Nooriafshar points out in an Australian study that learners "perceive that the learning process with an actual [human] teacher is more enjoyable than with a virtual [computer] teacher" (2012, 6), it can also be suggested that more flexibility is available to students with iPads who do not always have access to a human teacher. These students have a device that they can manipulate through touch and with the sound of their voice, as opposed to a laptop or desktop computer that must be manipulated with a keyboard and mouse and is not as easily transportable as a tablet-style learning device.

In conclusion, to state that the iPad and its counterparts are the key solutions to bringing equal and reliable access to education on a global level would not be fair or accurate. However, it would be equally unfair to assume that, because, like computers, these devices are expensive and complex, they would not be useful to increasing the breadth and depth of global education and awareness. The iPad is an excellent tool for flexibility in that it is a portable option (even if it is one of limited availability) that students and educators can use as a supplement to the core of their lessons. The personal electronic device in itself should be considered a tool to challenge the idea that education and intellectual freedom is not accessible in all parts of the world. Technology in most of its forms should be embraced, shared, and distributed throughout the global education system as much as possible but with caution and the awareness of how to use it as well as knowledge of its limitations and the consequences that may emerge from its use. These devices should not replace the tried-and-true methods that have been used to teach students for centuries; they should complement these methods in a way that provides as many options as possible so that as many people as possible, no matter where they are in the global community, can have access to intellectual freedom and growth.

References

Campante, Felipe R., and Davin Chor. 2012. "Why Was the Arab World Poised for Revolution? Schooling, Economic Opportunities, and the Arab Spring." *Journal of Economic Perspectives* 26(2): 167–187.

Crichton, Susan, Karen Pegler, and Duncan White. 2012. "Personal Devices in Public Settings: Lessons Learned From an iPod Touch/iPad Project." *Electric Journal of Elearning* 10(1): 23–31.

Ein-Dor, Phillip, Michael D. Myers, and K.S. Raman. 1997. "Information Technology in Three Small Developed Countries." *Journal of Management Information Systems* 13(4): 61–89.

Finkel, Donald L. *Teaching With Your Mouth Shut.* Portsmouth, NH: Boynton/Cook Publishers, 2000.

Fry, Stephen. "The iPad Launch: Can Steve Jobs Do It Again?" *Time Magazine,* April 1, 2010. www.time.com/time/magazine/article/0,9171,1977113,00.html.

Kassim, Saleem. 2012. "Twitter Revolution: How the Arab Spring Was Helped by Social Media." *PolicyMic.* www.policymic.com/articles/10642/twitter-revolution-how-the-arab-spring-was-helped-by-social-media.

Nooriafshar, Mehryar. 2012. "Educational Applications of the Emerging Technologies Available on Handheld Devices Such as iPad and iPhone." *Asian Journal of Management Sciences and Education* 1(1): 5–11.

Norris, Pippa. 2001. *Digital Divide: Civic Engagement, Information Poverty, and the Internet Worldwide (Communication, Society and Politics)*. Cambridge, UK: Cambridge University Press, 2001.

Pressler, Margaret Webb. 2004. "Textbook Prices on the Rise: Frequent New Editions, Supplemental Materials Drive Up Costs." *Washington Post*, September 18. www. washingtonpost.com/wp-dyn/articles/A30151-2004Sep17.html.

CHAPTER 6

From Traditional to Massive Online Education: The Global Health Village

Bernardo Ramirez, Maysoun Dimachkie Masri, and Cherie Lynn Ramirez

If you are a Baby Boomer, you have experienced the world going "global" in your lifetime. You likely remember your grandparents' stories about great changes during the early 20th century, including dramatic improvements in sanitation and the life-altering impact of new vaccines and antibiotics; occasional travels to distant places beyond their city of residence, and for the privileged, beyond their country or even continent; and the beginning of communication technologies, including radio and television. You also surely remember your parents marveling at innumerable signs of progress, including advances in medicine such as new treatments for cancer and heart disease; the advent of commercial air travel via those heavy, yet inexplicably reliable planes flying in just hours to remote corners of the world; and satellites in space marking the beginning of improved worldwide communication and rapidly updated news. The palpable interconnectedness of our lives has become a shared experience and perception in our lifetime.

We want to review here, as a case study, the progress made in teaching about health management and policy, highlighting the changes in educational methodologies and technologies, as well as the expansion of education beyond the traditional classroom to a global audience of facilitators and learners. As Salman Khan, founder of The Khan Academy, observes in *The One World Schoolhouse: Education Reimagined* (2012), the traditional way of teaching and learning does not fit well in the fast-changing global village. The new transformational model needs to stimulate a more proactive, flexible, and inclusive learning mode.

Education Beyond the Classroom

The technology revolution, which started with the improvement of communication and audiovisual technologies in the middle of the 20th century, has accelerated since the dawn of the internet. Commonplace and globalized access to the internet has forever changed our lives, and we will refer in this chapter mostly to the impact this has had on education and health. The basic premise has moved quickly from "How does a face-to-face interaction compare to one online?" to "How can we enhance our blended- or mixed-mode educational experiences?" Even if you are teaching a small group in a face-to-face situation, there may be room for enhancement by using multimedia. Through the power of such technologies, millions of viewers—and likely more than a few classrooms—have had global health professor Hans Rosling as a virtual guest speaker to dispel myths about trends in health and human development around the world (2006).

As we will see in specific examples in this chapter, Web 2.0 technologies have the potential to fortify learning experiences by reaching into new resources, media, and individuals, which by their diversely sourced nature makes the learning experience global. Table 6.1 lists some of the most commonly used technologies to support global educational collaborations that facilitate student-centered, problem-based learning.

Web 2.0 Technologies

Many of the Web 2.0 technologies used in education also have practical applications in the healthcare industry, justifying the exposure of healthcare management students to technologies that will yield substantial benefits both in the classroom and the workplace. These technologies have the potential to bring together faculty, students, health professionals, and health consumers to enhance learning, increase local and global collaboration, and ultimately create a quality healthcare system.

The U.S healthcare industry is facing challenges of epic proportions, with containing skyrocketing costs being a top priority ("Health Costs," 2012). On the front lines, managers of healthcare organizations are being asked to maintain high-quality and ever-changing standards while efficiently and effectively managing their limited resources. Providing quality and cost-effective healthcare requires that healthcare

Table 6.1   Technologies to Support Global Educational Collaborations

Category	Tool
Course management system	Blackboard (blackboard.com) Canvas by Instructure (canvas.instructure.com) Desire2Learn (desire2learn.com) Moodle (moodle.org) Sakaii (sakaiproject.org)
Self-guided learning platform	Articulate (articulate.com)
Web-based information sharing:	
Blogs	Blogger (blogger.com) WordPress (wordpress.com)
Digital storytelling	Flickr (flickr.com) VoiceThread (voicethread.com)
Educational videos	Khan Academy (khanacademy.org) iTunes (apple.com/itunes) YouTube (youtube.com)
Social bookmarking	CiteULike (citeulike.org) Delicious (delicious.com) LibraryThing (librarything.com)
Synchronous discussion:	
Videoconferencing	Google Hangouts (google.com/hangouts) Skype (skype.com)
Web-based chat	Piazza (piazza.com)
Web-based conference	Adobe Connect (adobe.com/products/adobeconnect.html) BigBlueButton (bigbluebutton.org) GoToMeeting (gotomeeting.com) ooVoo (oovoo.com) WebEx (webex.com)
Asynchronous or synchronous visual collaboration:	
Interactive whiteboards	Scriblink (scriblink.com)
Wikis	Etherpad (etherpad.org) PBworks (pbworks.com) Wikispaces (wikispaces.com)
Collaborative document editing	Dropbox (dropbox.com) Google Drive (drive.google.com)
Simulation	Open Cobalt (opencobalt.org) Second Life (secondlife.com)
Online survey interface	SurveyMonkey (surveymonkey.com)
Other asynchronous options	Discussion Boards Email Listservs Podcasting

organizations, managers, administrators, clinicians, and patients communicate and collaborate within the constraints of time and place.

Teaching healthcare management to graduate students and healthcare professionals requires the cultivation of advanced specialized skills through active learning and practical demonstration. Healthcare management educators are faced with a more mobile and technology-savvy student generation. Voice- and videoconferencing, chats, and emails are only some of the tools available to this generation. Web 2.0 technologies such as social networks, wikis, Twitter, and blogs can be brought into the classroom to bear on some of the challenges faced by faculty in enabling learners to succeed in the workplace and collaborate on the global level. This section offers a description of selected Web 2.0 technologies that were found to have a positive impact not only on the educational process of future healthcare managers but also on their professional development and their ability to connect to the real world of practice.

To learn more about the application of Web 2.0 technologies in empowering healthcare management students—such as increasing the probability of student academic and professional success, boosting the engagement of students in hybrid and online courses, or engaging alumni and community partners—let us first start by providing a formal definition. O'Reilly (Musser 2006) defines Web 2.0 technologies as "a set of economic, social, and technology trends that collectively form the basis for the next generation of the internet, a more mature, distinctive medium characterized by user participation, openness, and network effects." The main objectives of the use of Web 2.0 compared with Web 1.0 technologies are to increase communication, collaboration, and interaction (Van De Belt et al. 2010).

While Web 1.0 technologies allowed clinicians and health professionals to access medical information in the form of webpages, online journals, and databases, Web 2.0 technologies allow for the creation of user-generated healthcare content (McLean, Richards, & Wardman 2007). An illustrative example of Web 2.0 in health is HealthMap (healthmap.org), a web-based tool developed by a team of researchers, epidemiologists, and software developers at Boston Children's Hospital, which uses online informal sources for disease outbreak monitoring and real-time surveillance of emerging public health threats. A second example is the push toward electronic health records, which is expected to have a transformative effect on healthcare and may allow patients to become more active participants in their own care (Randeree 2009).

Facing the formidable task of preparing students for a world of complex health challenges, instructors can judiciously use Web 2.0 technologies to immerse students in problem-based learning, linking their understanding of their reality and learning needs with the knowledge and competency opportunities that they are exposed to during the learning experience (Engelhard & Seo 2012).

Examples of Web 2.0 Technologies

Social Media

People of all ages are using social media tools (e.g., texting, blogging, tagging, and emailing) and social networks (e.g., Facebook and Twitter) in their daily lives (Skelton 2012). As these tools continue to play a central role in shaping the communication channels between young adults, it seems beneficial to bring social media tools into the classroom. Social media can increase collaboration, information sharing, and innovation within a group of students even outside of the classroom.

Twitter

When teaching large classes (50 or more students), teachers face the challenge of engaging a significant number of students in a discussion. If all participants hypothetically wanted to be involved on a given day, there would likely not be enough time to accommodate everyone. By using Twitter, faculty can draw more students into the discussion in real time and provide a written record that can be reviewed or shared later.

Social Bookmarking

Social bookmarking provides a socially mediated channel for discovering and sharing information among group members. These tools enable users to create publicly viewable lists of bookmarks (i.e., a hyperlink to a sharable information resource) and typically also allow for the input of searchable keywords, or tags, for these bookmarks.

File-Sharing and Editing Platforms

Google Drive and Dropbox are two examples of tools that support collaborative work outside the classroom, by mediating secure yet easily accessible file-sharing. With Google Drive, multiple users can modify a document at once, a feature that is particularly useful for collaborative document-editing, such as data collection and report-writing.

Job Searching

The number of U.S. and multinational companies recruiting through social media is increasing (Jobvite 2011). These days, a person's digital profile is just another way to screen job applicants. Creating and maintaining a digital profile is becoming a de facto requirement for successful job search efforts. Students can link their digital profile to selected social media sites, such as Google, LinkedIn, and Facebook.

Blogs

A blog is essentially a discussion that you can publish to an audience of thousands (or more) worldwide. It consists of a number of posts listed in reverse chronological order that can be filtered by date, category, author, or other attributes. The blog administrator can invite and add other participants, whose permission and access are easily managed. There are millions of blogs of different shapes and sizes. Blogs help students organize, collect, collaborate, and share ideas with the world. Most importantly, the main objective in using a blog in academia is to engage students to read, reflect, criticize, question, and react to content posted by other bloggers. Since the posting is seen by an audience beyond their classmates, students tend to have greater consideration for the content and writing style.

Wikis

Wikis are ideal for group projects. The students are able to write and share in real time for a collaborative project, and the rest of the class and the instructor can also see the progress and provide feedback in a dynamic way if desired. Another advantage of wikis is that the authors can share their projects outside the class elearning platform. For example, students who are developing an analysis of the health sector of a given country can share their ideas and request information from real-life sources, including health ministry officials of that country, international experts, or consumers or providers of that particular health system. Wikis keep a record of the activity and the user that modified the document, which makes grading and assessing the individual and group effort easier and more transparent. Finally, wikis allow for creative expression, since the document can be designed as a webpage to include graphics, videos, and any form of creative communication.

Massive Open Online Courses

Massive open online courses, or MOOCs (rhymes with "dukes"), are a recent trend that has spread throughout the education world (Pappano 2012). These are essentially university courses that, for the most part, require no tuition payment and do not provide credit, and anyone with access to the internet can enroll in them. The basic idea is that a "massive" number of learners join this common internet-based platform and engage in a learning experience, typically with classmates from all over the world (Figure 6.1).

Canvas (Figure 6.2), Coursera, Udacity, and edX[1] are among the most popular MOOC platforms at the time of this writing. Using the principles of the "flipped classroom" that have been promoted by Khan ("Let's Use Video to Reinvent Education" 2011), most of these courses deliver basic knowledge content thorough short videos, videotaped

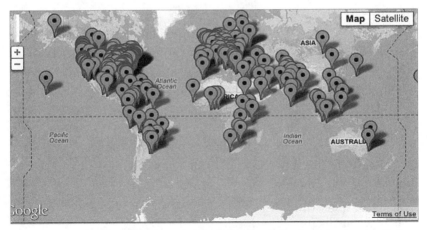

Figure 6.1   The broad geographical distribution of students enrolled in Canvas's Spring 2013 International Health Systems course, led by Dr. Bernardo Ramirez of the University of Central Florida

Figure 6.2　A sampling of upcoming courses from Canvas as of December 2012

face-to-face classes, webinars, or PowerPoint presentations with sound. The course may be led by one or more faculty members from across the globe who develop learning environments to engage students in small group discussions. Videoconference presentations and discussions presented and conducted by the learners themselves stimulate their analytic skills. Participants may respond to quizzes to confirm their knowledge or engage in case studies, simulations, projects, or papers to demonstrate the application of their knowledge to solve practical problems in the real world.

The power of MOOCs to transform higher education is not without challenges, including:

- *High attrition rates*: Signing up for these courses is relatively easy, so participants can be extremely heterogeneous—ranging from students of all levels to faculty, professionals, and anyone else. Although this is one of the great strengths of truly accessible learning, some participants will inevitably be unprepared for their academic load or may become otherwise unable to complete course requirements, leading to high attrition rates and low course completion rates (Kolowich 2013).

- *Lack of resources and access*: Although tuition is no longer a barrier with most MOOCs, some participants may still lack access to the required online technologies or academic resource materials, such as textbooks and libraries with scholarly sources. This may also occur without warning, as when the Pakistani government shut down access to YouTube in September 2012, leaving online learners who relied on it suddenly in the dark (Ripley 2012). A related issue is the potentially exclusionary requirement for high-speed internet connections to enable the use of synchronous communication with video and multiple users.

- *Limited interaction with faculty*: The instructor-to-student ratio and the medium make it impossible for traditional personal interactions to occur (e.g., purposeful and often time-consuming interventions to help struggling students one-on-one). These are replaced by computer-graded quizzes, peer-reviewed assignments, and discussion interactions mostly with other participants. However, if well-managed, these elements can still lead to very enriching learning experiences.

- *No credit*: Due to a variety of logistical and political reasons, these courses do not currently provide academic credit, so other incentives have been developed to provide motivation for enrollment and reward the effort these courses require (Lewin 2012). One incentive system that has been developed involves badges, which were inspired by achievement emblems used by the Boy Scouts and video games and are currently being developed by Mozilla Open Badges

(Young 2012). Some speculate these badges will be a more accurate indicator of competencies achieved by learners for potential employers than more traditional measures, such as grade point averages.

- *Communication barriers*: With students signing in from the most remote parts of the world, some challenges will require carefully crafted solutions. One issue is the lack of multilingual learning platforms to facilitate the full expression of learners in their own language. This problem is currently being circumvented by offering most courses in English, expecting that a larger number of participants will take the courses. However, with the current and potential capacities of digital translators, such as Google Translate, a multilingual online platform to enhance participant learning interactions seems closer to reality.

Despite some of these potential shortcomings, there are also unexpected advantages that may make the value of MOOCs even greater than originally envisioned. One is the ability to use this laboratory for performing large-scale experiments to optimize learning platforms, teaching strategies, and assessment tools. Some of these insights may be instructive even for non–web-based instruction and the study of human cognition.

Conclusion

Web 2.0 technologies, including MOOCs, have irreversibly changed the way we think about education (Davidson 2012). Now these tools must be harnessed to further increase our familiarity and proficiency with creating effective learning experiences and to ensure access to this knowledge for all populations.

Just when we think we understand a problem—whether in education or health—and its solutions, the pace of ongoing transformations accelerates and new variants appear, some of them perhaps generated by solutions previously implemented. These situations can be stimulating, yet also very frustrating. In the quest for continuous improvement of processes and resources for learning, the only constant is change and the most practical tool is an innovative spirit.

Endnote

1. URLs and short descriptions for these and other resources can be found in the appendix at the end of the chapter.

References

Davidson, Cathy N. 2012. "Size Isn't Everything: For Academe's Future, Think Mash-Ups Not MOOCs." *The Chronicle of Higher Education*. December 10. chronicle.com/article/Size-Isnt-Everything/136153/?cid=cr&utm_source=cr&utm_medium=en.

Engelhard, Chalee, and Kay Kyeong-Ju Seo. 2012. "Going From Obsolete to Innovative: Empowering Problem-Based Learning With Online Social Media." In *Designing Problem-Driven Instruction With Online Social Media*, edited by Kay Kyeong-Ju Seo, Debra A. Pellegrino, and Chalee Engelhard, 3–20. Charlotte, NC: Information Age Publishing Inc.

"Health Costs." 2012. The Henry J. Kaiser Family Foundation. kff.org/health-costs.

Jobvite. 2011. *Social Recruiting Survey Results*. web.jobvite.com/rs/jobvite/images/Jobvite-SRP-2011.pdf.

Khan, Salman. 2012. *The One World Schoolhouse: Education Reimagined*. New York: Grand Central Publishing.

Kolowich, Steve. 2013. "Coursera Takes a Nuanced View of MOOC Dropout Rates." *The Chronicle of Higher Education*. April 8. chronicle.com/blogs/wiredcampus/coursera-takes-a-nuanced-view-of-mooc-dropout-rates/43341.

"Let's Use Video to Reinvent Education: Salman Khan on TED.com." 2011. *TED Blog*. blog.ted.com/2011/03/09/lets-use-video-to-reinvent-education-salman-khan-on-ted-com/.

Lewin, Tamar. 2012. "College Credit Eyed for Online Courses." *New York Times*. November 13. www.nytimes.com/2012/11/14/education/moocs-to-be-evaluated-for-possible-college-credit.html.

McLean, Rick, Brian H. Richards, and Janet I. Wardman. 2007. "The Effect of Web 2.0 on the Future of Medical Practice and Education: Darwikinian Evolution or Folksonomic Revolution?" *Medical Journal of Australia* 187(3): 174–177.

Musser, John (with Tim O'Reilly and the O'Reilly Radar Team). 2006. O'Reilly Radar: *Web 2.0 Principles and Best Practices*. radar.oreilly.com/2006/11/web-20-principles-and-best-pra.html.

Pappano, Laura. 2012. "The Year of the MOOC." *New York Times*. November 2. www.nytimes.com/2012/11/04/education/edlife/massive-open-online-courses-are-multiplying-at-a-rapid-pace.html?ref=edlife.

Randeree, Ebrahim. 2009. "Exploring Technology Impacts of Healthcare 2.0 Initiatives." *Telemedicine Journal and e-Health* 15(3): 255–260.

Ripley, Amanda. 2012. "College Is Dead. Long Live College!" *Time*. October 18. nation.time.com/2012/10/18/college-is-dead-long-live-college.

Rosling, Hans. 2006. "The Best Stats You've Ever Seen." TED. www.ted.com/talks/hans_rosling_shows_the_best_stats_you_ve_ever_seen.html.

Skelton, Alissa. 2012. "Social Demographics: Who's Using Today's Biggest Networks." *Mashable*. March 9. mashable.com/2012/03/09/social-media-demographics.

Van De Belt, Tom H., Lucien J. Engelen, Sivera A.A. Berben, and Lisette Schoonhoven. 2010. "Definition of Health 2.0 and Medicine 2.0: A Systematic Review." *Journal of Medical Internet Research*, 12(2): e18.

Young, Jeffrey R. 2012. "'Badges' Earned Online Pose Challenge to Traditional College Diplomas." *The Chronicle of Higher Education*. January 8. chronicle.com/article/Badges-Earned-Online-Pose/130241.

Appendix

Annotated References: Internet Platforms for MOOCs and Related References

- Canvas (canvas.net): "Canvas Network gives teachers, learners, and institutions alike the place and platform to define the world of open online learning in a way that makes sense for everyone. It grows as teachers and learners apply it in individual ways and then share the results with the world."

- Coursera (coursera.org):"We are a social entrepreneurship company that partners with the top universities in the world to offer courses online for anyone to take, for free. We envision a future where the top universities are educating not only thousands of students, but millions. Our technology enables the best professors to teach tens or hundreds of thousands of students. Through this, we hope to give everyone access to the world-class education that has so far been available only to a select few. We want to empower people with education that will improve their lives, the lives of their families, and the communities they live in."

- EdX (edx.org): "EdX is a not-for-profit enterprise of its founding partners Harvard University and the Massachusetts Institute of Technology that features learning designed specifically for interactive study via the web. Based on a long history of collaboration and their shared educational missions, the founders are creating a new online-learning experience with online courses that reflect their disciplinary breadth. Along with offering online courses, the institutions will use edX to research how students learn and how technology can transform learning–both on-campus and worldwide."

- Health 2.0 (health2con.com): "Health 2.0 promotes, showcases, and catalyzes new technologies in healthcare. We do this through a worldwide series of conferences, code-a-thons, prize challenges, and more. We also have the leading market intelligence on new health technology companies."

- Jobvite (jobvite.com): "Jobvite is the leading recruiting platform for the social web. Social recruiting products from Jobvite lead the market in their proven ability to drive referral hires. Jobvite Source is the social recruiting and candidate relationship management application that targets relevant talent in LinkedIn, Facebook, and Twitter to drive referral hiring virally. From social referral to interview management to advanced analytics, Jobvite Hire is the faster, more productive way for everyone to work together."

- The Khan Academy (khanacademy.org):"The Khan Academy is an organization on a mission. We're a not-for-profit with the goal of changing education for the better by providing a free world-class education for anyone anywhere. All of the site's resources are available to anyone. It doesn't matter if you are a student, teacher, home-schooler, principal, adult returning to the classroom after 20 years, or a friendly alien just trying to get a leg up in earthly biology. The Khan Academy's materials and resources are available to you completely free of charge."

- MERLOT: Multimedia Educational Resource for Learning and Online Teaching (merlot.org/merlot/

index.htm): MERLOT is a free and open online
community of resources designed primarily for faculty,
staff, and students of higher education from around the
world to share their learning materials and pedagogy.
MERLOT is a leading-edge, user-centered collection
of peer-reviewed higher education, online learning
materials, catalogued by registered members and a set of
faculty development support services."

• Mozilla Open Badges (openbadges.org): "Mozilla's
Open Badge Infrastructure provides the open, core
technology to support an ecosystem of badges. It is
designed to support a broad range of different badge
issuers, and allow any user to earn badges across
different issuers, websites, and experiences, then
combine them into a single collection tied to their
identity. This collection of badges can then be shared
[with] various audiences across the web, resulting in
real-world results like jobs or formal credit." Read about
Mozilla Wiki Badges at wiki.mozilla.org/badges.

• Udacity (udacity.com): "We believe university-level
education can be both high quality and low cost. Using
the economics of the internet, we've connected some of
the greatest teachers to hundreds of thousands of students
in almost every country on Earth. Udacity was founded
by three roboticists who believed much of the educational
value of their university classes could be offered online for
very low cost. A few weeks later, over 160,000 students
in more than 190 countries enrolled in our first class,
'Introduction to Artificial Intelligence.' The class was
twice profiled by the *New York Times* and also by other
news media. Now we're a growing team of educators and
engineers, on a mission to change the future of education."

CHAPTER 7

Teacher ePortfolios: Links to Interpersonal and Intrapersonal 21st-Century Communication Skills

Eunice M. Merideth and Peggy E. Steinbronn

The current trend toward the use of ePortfolios for assessment and accreditation provides programs with a reliable tool for measuring what their candidates know and are able to do as they finish their programs. Beyond an assessment tool, however, an ePortfolio is also a communication medium for 21st-century skills—a way for teacher candidates to step out and share accomplishments, contact prospective employers globally and market themselves anywhere the internet extends, and reflect on what has been done in the past in order to improve what will be in the future. These links to interpersonal and intrapersonal communication provide development in 21st-century information, communications, and technology (ITC) literacy.

It is true that a traditional résumé and portfolio foster communication by providing an input–output medium as a record of education and a documentation of experiences. An electronic portfolio, however, moves one step beyond by "showing" in addition to "telling." Instructional methods come alive, as lesson plans can be linked to interactive materials and videos. In addition, the application of those methods can be analyzed through reflections as students learn from their own teaching. In this way, the knowledge and skills as defined by current Interstate Teacher Assessment and Support Consortium (InTASC) Standards have become central to structuring an ePortfolio for a midsize liberal arts university's school of education, even as the reflections about each of these standards has developed stronger pedagogy. Tracy Penny

Light and colleagues (2012) suggest that ePortfolios also contribute to creative and critical thinking in that they are a "richer representation of the learners' experiences" (61).

When teacher candidates infuse these ePortfolios with newer Web 2.0 technology, such as VoiceThreads (voicethread.com), video clips, images, and student work samples, they are also creating links for learning for themselves and their future K–12 students. Cultural theorist Henry Jenkins (2006) asserts that controlling media in different ways for communication creates a convergence culture: "Convergence represents a paradigm shift—a move from medium-specific content toward content that flows across multiple media channels, toward the increased interdependence of communication styles" (243). While an ePortfolio creates its own challenges in process, the product takes up little physical space, can be accessed with little effort, and serves as a bridge to connect anyone who has internet access with the author.

In addition to knowledge and skills that exhibit content, teaching, learning, and assessment, an ePortfolio can also illustrate teaching dispositions. Paul Watkins and Ruth Ann Roberts (2009) report that the application of audio, video, and photography "provide evidence of teacher creativity, caring, and personality. Such positive traits underpin the portfolio as evidence of professional and personal ethics and affect" (3). This kind of communication is valuable as interpersonal communication for others, but it is vital in developing self-perception.

The purpose of this chapter is to explore the methodology being used to build a multimedia ePortfolio for candidates in a teacher education program that encourages both interpersonal and intrapersonal communication for learning—communication strategies that can literally be used any time and anywhere in the world. Moreover, this chapter will report results from quantitative measures of students engaged in creating such portfolios and qualitative contributions from two students who used their ePortfolios to reach across the world and obtain international teaching positions.

Methodology of Building and Assessing the ePortfolio as a Communication Tool

The ePortfolio Project described herein was first instituted in the fall of 2008 and has been an important part of program continuity and assessment since that time. It was designed to strengthen teaching candidates and support their education program by providing students with a software medium (LiveText) for a personal learning environment (PLE) that fields the electronic portfolio as well as unlimited storage space on the web in a cloud computing format. First introduced by Jeremy Hiebert (2006) from British Columbia, a PLE is a type of learning for and by the student using "pulled information" instead of "pushed information." Pulled information is data that a student gathers and stores, instead of being a passive receiver of information that is simply given, or pushed. The environment can also be used to store pushed information, of course, but the point is that the student is in charge. Jay Simmons (1996) describes the act of collecting information as a three-step process of collection, reflection, and selection. We have adopted this process as the inputs into our PLE. This also means that the student is responsible for developing and maintaining this environment so that it reflects what the student selects to save and store. The model for the PLE (Figure 7.1) is introduced with LiveText software in the foundations class, and students are asked to complete assignments in LiveText and save them along with other relevant information in preparation for creating an ePortfolio as a summative assessment and career entry vehicle at the end of their program.

Ongoing support for the PLE of students is extended throughout the program as students complete InTASC target assignments within this environment, use modules developed for them to collect information about practicum placements and hours served before student teaching, and learn to create and use Web 2.0 technologies. Ron Lubensky (2006) explains how a PLE helps link a student's learning experiences over

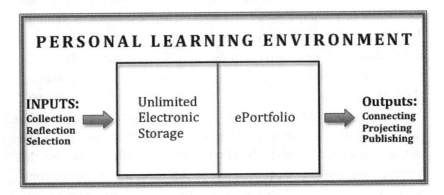

Figure 7.1   PLE model (©2010 Merideth and Steinbronn)

time by bringing artifacts together in one space: "A [PLE] is a facility for an individual to access, aggregate, configure, and manipulate digital artifacts of their ongoing learning experiences" (para. 3). Graham Attwell (2007) explains that PLEs can also increase accountability, as the holistic environments bring together separate sources and contexts: "PLEs provide learners with their own spaces under their own control to develop and share ideas. ... Students learn how to take responsibility for their own learning" (7).

Moving the PLE to an ePortfolio format occurs within the student teaching semester. Because students are busy throughout the week in their classrooms, we have elected to bring them in for 2 weekend days—one at the beginning of the semester and one toward the end. This is the place where students use their materials stored in the PLE and add materials created and used in student teaching. Again, the learner is in control. At this point, the learner chooses the content that he or she wishes to include, the style or appearance of the portfolio, and who may interact with the content (Severance, Hardin, and Whyte 2008).

Students meet in a seminar format twice during the course of the semester and keep in contact with the instructor throughout in an online format using the university's course management system. The content of the seminar includes discussion, a writing workshop to identify and practice descriptive and reflective writing, and a variety of Web 2.0 technologies that allow students to embed multimedia content into their ePortfolio. Support and frequent feedback from the instructor are necessary components to keep students moving toward their ePortfolio completion in a timely manner. The use of LiveText as the medium for the ePortfolio provides a standard of delivery and, at the same time, allows students to be creative in how they choose to present their PLE.

Although the use of a standard set of templates provides a starting place, the end results are anything but standard. Students bring their own uniqueness to the ePortfolio and give it their own "brand" or style. However, creative freedom is not the same thing as "running wild." The instructor applies a rubric to the ePortfolio components throughout the semester, designed to assess the components at various stages of completion to ensure that all students meet the standards and expectations of the program.

The use of multimedia is encouraged as its use helps provide a more complete and accurate picture of what actually happened in the classroom. Web 2.0 technologies such as VoiceThread, Pho.to (pho.to), and Scribd (scribd.com) provide a quick and easy way for students to include more visual and auditory elements to their selected artifacts, and they are available any time and any place as long as there is an active internet connection. These Web 2.0 tools are also easily transferred for use by preservice teachers to students in their own K–12 classrooms and provide evidence to prospective employers that applicants possess sophisticated and current 21st-century technology skills.

In a recent global study that spanned 24 schools in seven countries to explore the teaching practices that enable student learning of 21st-century skills, Linda Shear and Larry Gallagher (2012) found that "in most settings, teachers' use of technology for teaching was far more common than students' use of technology for learning … with technology available in the classroom before related curricular materials and models for its powerful and effective use were." Their suggestions for improving technological teaching and learning in countries from Finland and Australia to Senegal and Indonesia included technological opportunities for students to develop 21st-century communication and problem-solving skills and extending learning opportunities with technology. Structuring a personal learning environment that integrates different communication skills into a final product such as an ePortfolio would provide strategies such as these as well as a product for student use and assessment.

As part of their publication within their PLE, students at our university are encouraged to use their completed ePortfolio as a tool in their applications for teaching positions. During the second seminar session, students create a business card with the access information about their ePortfolio to send out with any teaching applications. The business card includes the student's name, contact information, and the link to the student's ePortfolio with instructions for logging in with a private code. This also provides a way for students to connect with other professionals/prospective employers who may be interested in seeing evidence of a student's teaching accomplishments. It provides a way to publish and showcase evidence of teaching practice by a preservice teacher. While the primary purpose of the ePortfolio in this program is meeting program standards and understanding and reflecting upon the artifacts presented to complete program goals, a by-product is continued professional growth that synchronizes with career goals and provides a tool for marketing oneself to potential employers. The synthesis that occurs within the ePortfolio transitions well to any interview process. Students are able to "talk the talk," providing the job interviewer with a clear understanding of their teaching journey as well as current knowledge, skills, and dispositions.

Assessment Results

General Program Assessment

General program assessment using ePortfolios has provided aggregated data across the entire program for the first time, allowing faculty members to assess curriculum with real data. As faculty members assess our students' ePortfolios in the students' content areas, reports generated can highlight areas of strength and those curriculum areas that need to be strengthened. For example, in Figure 7.2, in the fall of 2009, the analysis of ePortfolio assessments for that semester indicated a weakness in Standards 3 and 7. Steps were taken to strengthen these areas within the program immediately.

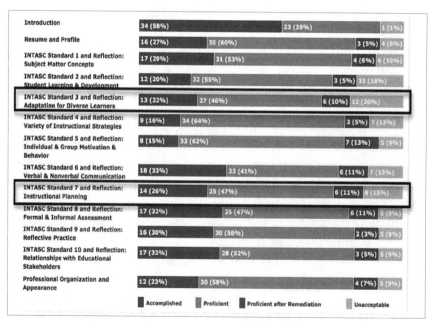

Figure 7.2 ePortfolio assessment results for Fall 2009

Figure 7.3 illustrates the difference a year makes when a program pays attention to this type of data. For the fall of 2010, the weaknesses have diminished significantly, because of program adjustment and student alignment.

This type of direct link with students' artifacts and reflections is obviously helpful to the program in examining curriculum and encouraging sustainability of resources. But what of the students' perceptions? Because we wanted to determine what types of ICT communication students found helpful both in completing the process and creating the product of an ePortfolio, we surveyed 76 students in the spring of 2011. The response rate from this survey was 91 percent, or 69 respondents, across five programs that result in licensure: undergraduate elementary education (ELED), undergraduate secondary education (SEED), undergraduate music education, graduate master of arts (MAT) in teaching for secondary certification, and graduate master of science in teaching (MST) for elementary certification. Table 7.1 provides a summary of these items aggregated and then disaggregated by program.

Results within Table 7.1 indicate strong support for the ePortfolio as a communication tool across all programs, but it is strongest in secondary programs at the undergraduate and graduate levels. Support is weaker in the MST program and music programs, which may be

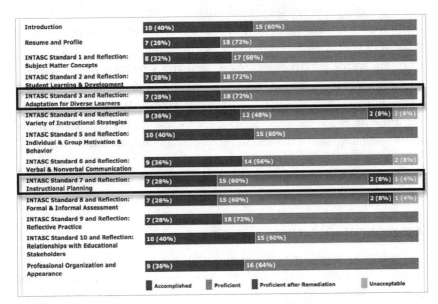

Figure 7.3   ePortfolio assessment results for Fall 2010

Table 7.1 ePortfolio Survey Results in Spring 2011

Survey Items	Aggregated Data (n=69)		Elementary UG, (n=19)		Secondary UG, (n=28)		Music UG, (n=6)		MAT Grad, (n=10)		MST Grad, (n=6)	
	Mean	Median	Mean	Median	Mean	Median	Mean	Median	Mean	Median	Mean	Median
An ePortfolio is a good vehicle for showcasing my work.	4.42	5.0	4.26	4.0	4.61	5.0	4.17	4.0	4.5	4.5	4.33	4.0
An ePortfolio can be used to demonstrate knowledge, skills, and understanding.	4.33	4.0	4.11	4.0	4.54	5.0	4.33	4.0	4.4	4.0	4.0	4.0
I have wider communication possibilities because of my ePortfolio.	3.75	4.0	3.32	4.0	3.86	4.5	3.67	4.0	4.4	4.5	3.67	3.5
My ePortfolio has helped me reflect about my program and preparation to be a teacher.	4.13	4.0	3.79	4.0	4.32	4.0	4.33	4.0	4.3	4.5	3.83	4.0
The use of an ePortfolio will be useful in my future teaching career.	3.91	4.0	3.74	4.0	4.07	4.0	4.0	4.0	4.2	4.0	3.17	3.0
How would you rate the ePortfolio as a tool to help you prepare for a job interview?	3.81	4.0	3.58	4.0	4.0	4.5	3.5	3.0	4.3	5.0	3.17	3.0

Likert Scale 1–5: 1=Strongly Disagree; 2=Disagree; 3=Neither Agree or Disagree; 4=Agree; 5=Strongly Agree

related to fewer technology experiences within these programs. The highest aggregated mean (4.42/5.0) and median (5.0/5.0) illustrate most students' confidence that the ePortfolio will communicate their work to others. Even the lowest combined mean (3.75/5.0) is a strong measure of students asserting that they have wider communication possibilities because of the ePortfolio.

In addition to the quantitative measures surveyed and reported, students were asked to respond to the prompt, "What strengths do you see in creating and sending an ePortfolio to prospective employers?" Responses were categorized as positive, negative, or neutral. There were very few negative replies submitted, as illustrated in Table 7.2.

In the spring of 2012, we again surveyed graduates of the teacher education program but sought more qualitative measures so that we were sure we were hearing the students' voices. We focused on two main questions: 1. Please offer comments about your electronic portfolio and its value in documenting your accomplishment of InTASC Standards 1–10; and 2. Please offer comments about your electronic portfolio and its value in collecting, selecting, and presenting reflective writing. Results of that survey appear in Table 7.3.

Assessment With Global Implications

In his article "Five Technology Skills for the Global Economy," Dan Tynan (2006) stresses that technology is one key to succeeding in an emerging global economy. Among the five skills he found most important were: "distance management, independent thinking, creativity,

Table 7.2   Results of Qualitative Questions in Spring 2011

Program	Number of Positive Replies	Percentage of Positive Replies	Sample Reply
ELED	15/19	79%	I love the ability to look deeper into the standards and really see how they have applied in my teaching. The ways in which I was able to comprehend the standards more was all thanks to this program.
SEED	20/28	71%	I see my portfolio as a great way to prepare for future interviews. I find it is a great way for me to organize my thoughts. This can help me narrow my focus and prepare me to say exactly what I need to because I have been planning and preparing this portfolio for months. I can also whip out facts and examples without hesitation.
Music	6/6	100%	Showcases my skills and knowledge as a teacher through various mediums.
MAT (graduate secondary)	8/10	80%	Enhanced information sharing that will never get lost or ruined. A professional way to showcase my work.
MST (graduate elementary)	5/6	83%	Employers have a chance to see a picture of you, know that you are technologically savvy, and have a clear understanding of effective teaching concepts.

Table 7.3   Results of Qualitative Questions in Spring 2012

Questions	Positive Replies	Neutral Replies	Negative Replies	Sample Reply
Question 1 n=46	32	7	7	The ePortfolio was extremely important for me in documenting the InTASC Standards. The organization was perfect, and the navigation was extremely user-friendly. I can't imagine a better way to have done my final portfolio.
Question 2 n=44	33	3	8	I really think it is a useful 21st-century tool. It forces you to embrace technology, reflect about what you have done in the program, and have an organized, focused tool that helps drive you in the job interview.

cultural sensitivity, and language skills." In order to test the viability of ePortfolios in helping attain these skills, we conducted a case study of two graduates who used their ePortfolio to obtain international teaching jobs. A case study such as this analyzes a limited number of events or conditions in their real-world context. In this case, two graduated students (Subject A=SA and Subject B=SB) had taken teaching positions across the world, in China and in Hong Kong, respectively. Both SA and SB indicated that they used the internet more than 2 hours every day and strongly agreed that their PLEs were good places to store and showcase materials from their former classes and experiences and to collect current materials and revise their ePortfolios. When asked what types of multimedia were used in their ePortfolios, there were similarities as well as a more robust use of Web 2.0 by SB, as seen in Table 7.4.

Table 7.4   Types of Multimedia Used in ePortfolio

Subjects	Types of Multimedia
SA	Lesson plans, rubrics, reflections, visuals, PowerPoint presentations, PDF scanned personal documents, PDF scanned student work, Excel charts
SB	Lesson plans, rubrics, reflections, visuals, PowerPoint presentations, video clips, PDF scanned student work, authored WebQuest, live links, VoiceThreads

When asked about communication skills and creativity, SA stated the following:

> I believe the ePortfolio has given me a way to compile my strengths and talents and present them in a professional manner. The portfolio displays a work product that cannot be evaluated in a 1 to 3 hour job interview. I feel that my portfolio expresses a great deal of insight on not only my work, but also upon my individual beliefs and overall character.

SB's answer to this question indicates a more pragmatic approach:

> I believe the portfolio is efficient and cost-effective, especially since I sent it internationally. It is a more dynamic "introduction" that supports the usual cover letter and résumé. It also demonstrates that, as a teacher, I am tech-savvy.

When asked to give an open comment, SA provided an insight into the contributions of an ePortfolio to intrapersonal reflection and independent thinking:

> Through the use of the ePortfolio, I have been able to reflect on my own strengths and weaknesses. Having the ability to constantly check up on my work and add new samples and ideas or even update the old has been very beneficial to me

as an educator. I am constantly learning something new, and an ePortfolio has given me a way to express those beliefs and practices in a personal way.

In this section of the interview, SB's comments focused on how the ePortfolio process can help support synthesis and establish credibility:

The ePortfolio does not need to feel overwhelming during student teaching; it needs to be approached/supported/ incorporated throughout education courses, so that students can understand that the ePortfolio is intended to assist them in demonstrating what they know. ePortfolios could be likened to the special suits that U.S. Olympic swimmers use in competitions: They make great candidates even greater and help boost performance amidst stiff competition.

After a year of international teaching, both SA and SB indicate that they are still using their ePortfolios as a reflective tool and will use them to launch even more exciting teaching adventures as they seek further international teaching positions. In the past 2 years, 15 students from this program have obtained international teaching positions.

Discussion and Implications

Twenty-first century ICT skills encompass the application of technology as a tool to research, organize, evaluate, and communicate information. With its emphasis on student control of inputs (collection, reflection, and selection) and construction of a variety of outputs (connecting, projecting, and publishing), a PLE resulting in an ePortfolio provides both practice and products that first develop and then demonstrate these skills. The ePortfolio, however, need not be the end product; rather, it can be a transition to continued learning beyond formal education, to reflection after implementation, to multiple means of expression, and to connecting resources as well as people, both nationally and internationally: "To be effective in the 21st century, citizens and workers must be able to exhibit a range of functional and critical thinking skills related to information, media, and technology" ("Information, Media, and Technology Skills" 2007). From this perspective, ePortfolios may also prepare users to deal with changing dynamics and the exciting technologies of the future.

George Siemens (2004) reports that ePortfolios offer many benefits for learners as they create and reflect:

- Manage personal knowledge

- Provide a history of development and growth

- Supply a tool for planning and goal-setting

- Assist learners in making connections between learning experiences

- Provide the metacognitive elements needed to assist learners in planning future learning needs based on previous successes and failures

- Take personal control of learning history

Results reported in this chapter indicate that the teacher education students surveyed both in the United States and in international settings support these elements. Success with the adoption and implementation of ePortfolios in this program has been sustained by building ICT skills in the following manner:

- Students are introduced to the software and the concept of a PLE and 21st-century communication skills early in their program during the foundations class. Within this experience, they load examples into the software's file manager so that they collect and select resources as they begin their journey.

- Target assignments throughout the program are loaded into the students' PLE, but the platform is not limited to just course assignments. Students are encouraged to collect information that is relevant to them so that they will have a variety of materials from which to select for their ePortfolios. They are also taught how to do reflective writing so that it moves from a description of the present to a projection of future use.

- An open lab is offered every week for 90 minutes so that students can receive help on any of the web tools they will be using as well as the web-based software that hosts the process and ePortfolio.

- During the ePortfolio seminar, taken while student teaching, students continue the selection process and reflect upon the implementation of the materials selected. This seminar, taught by an educational technology expert, also allows students to get help with Web 2.0 applications and polish their publication efforts.

- The LiveText software license that students use for their PLEs, including the ePortfolio, extends for 1 year beyond graduation, so students can continue to use the software and university-produced templates. They may also continue to use the software after 1 year for a nominal yearly fee.

- From a programmatic point of view, faculty involvement with assignments and InTASC Standards assessment ensures the sustainability of the process across semesters and programs while providing data for continuing curricular improvement.

While past successes can be celebrated, there are certainly implications for moving forward. For example, John Zubizarreta (2009) describes the primary motive for a learning portfolio as the ability "to improve student learning by providing a structure for students to reflect systematically over time on the learning process and to develop the aptitudes, skills, and habits that come from critical reflection" (19). Therefore, the implications associated with this process would include the following:

1. Adopt the PLE/ePortfolio early in the program so that students have a chance to develop the technological skill to collect, store, and publish their results.

2. Establish the difference between descriptive and reflective writing early.

3. Encourage students to take ownership of their PLE and ePortfolios for personal choice and personalized learning.

4. Understand that PLEs/ePortfolios lead to a more meaningful engagement with content and pedagogy.

5. Promote faculty involvement with the process throughout a student's program so that they might help scaffold student knowledge and skills within content and pedagogical areas.

6. Provide one-on-one support sessions as well as clear directions about how to manage the technology.

7. Help students commit to this process as the first step in their own continued learning as well as an application for use in K–12 classrooms.

These implications are relevant in a global sense because the technology that enables bridges that connect one person to another can span nations and even continents, creating international outreach. The skills acquired by creating and developing a PLE—independent thinking and learning, collecting, reflecting, selecting, connecting, projecting, and publishing—are skills that benefit anyone in the world. Indeed, Attwell (2007) asserts that a "PLE is comprised of all the different tools we use in our everyday life for learning" (4). PLEs do not differentiate between formal learning and informal learning—there is only learning. They also provide learners with their own control and spaces to share their ideas.

Eva Heinrich and colleagues (2007) maintain that the process of creating a PLE and presenting an electronic portfolio has value "to develop and demonstrate lifelong learning skills" (660). It is through the interpersonal and intrapersonal 21st-century communication skills of self-assessment, reflection, and sharing that one learns to adapt, to become aware of relationships, and to set new goals—making learning relevant throughout life.

References

Attwell, Graham. 2007. "Personal Learning Environments—The Future of eLearning?" *eLearning Papers*, 2(1): 1–8.

Heinrich, Eva, Madhumita Bhattacharya, and Rayudu Ramesh. 2007. "Preparation for Lifelong Learning Using ePortfolios." *European Journal of Engineering Education*, 32(6): 653–663.

Hiebert, Jeremy. 2006. Personal Learning Environment Model." *HeadsPace J.* February 17. headspacej.blogspot.com/2006/02/personal-learning-environment-model.html [*URL no longer available*].

"Information, Media, and Technology Skills." 2007. *Route 21*. www.p21.org/route21/index.php?Itemid=8&id=2&option=com_content&view=article.

Jenkins, Henry. 2006. *Convergence Culture: Where Old and New Media Collide.* New York: New York University Press.

Light, Tracy Penny, Helen L. Chen, and John C. Ittelson. 2012. *Documenting Learning With ePortfolios: A Guide for College Instructors.* San Francisco: Jossey-Bass.

Lubensky, Ron. 2006. "The Present and Future of Personal Learning Environments." *Deliberations*. www.deliberations.com.au/2006/12/present-and-future-of-personal-learning.html.

Severance, Charles, Joseph Hardin, and Anthony Whyte. (2008). "The Coming Functionality Mash-Up in Personal Learning Environments. *Interactive Learning Environments*, 16(1), 47–62.

Shear, Linda, and Larry Gallagher. 2012. "Innovation Abroad, Insight at Home." *T.H.E. Journal.* October 9. thejournal.com/articles/2012/10/09/innovation-abroad-insight-at-home.aspx.

Siemens, George. 2004. "ePortfolios." *elearnspace*. December 16. elearnspace.org/Articles/eportfolios.htm.

Simmons, Jay. 1996. "Control the Purpose, Not the Contents: Coaching the Creation of Teaching Portfolios in Teacher Education." *Action in Teacher Education*, 18(1): 71–81.

Tynan, Dan. 2006. "Five Technology Skills for the Global Economy." InfoWorld. May 22. infoworld.com/t/business/five-technology-skills-global-economy-166.

Watkins, Paul, and Ruth Ann Roberts. 2009. "Multidimensional Recruiting: Electronic Evidence Breaking Traditions." *International Journal of Educational Leadership Preparation*, 4(3). cnx.org/content/m31929/latest.

Zubizarreta, John. 2009. *The Learning Portfolio: Reflective Practice for Improving Student Learning*, 2nd ed. San Francisco: Jossey-Bass.

CHAPTER 8

Furthering Educational Technology in Developing Countries

Carrie Schulz

The idea of bringing educational technology into developing countries has always been appealing. In developed countries, we have seen the effect technology can have on enhancing education. The natural desire is to bring these opportunities to others. The field of educational technology and the need are so broad that it makes it difficult to conceptualize how to do this.

When working within a developing country, sustainability needs to be at the core of your approach. Quite often we see organizations impacting schools and educational facilities around the world with approaches that are impossible for the local organizations to maintain. When this happens, the effect of the work is limited; frequently it expires once the group or implementer leaves. Taking a systematic approach when embarking upon a project such as this can help make the project successful. This chapter will evaluate key issues to consider, demonstrate how to identify a focus, and take readers through recent plan development and implementation. Finally, we will discuss how to keep the work moving forward to help the organization progress further. I will use several references to a project a colleague and I worked on, which involved bringing a group of college students to Abaco, Bahamas, in 2009 to introduce educational technology into a school for children with disabilities. The school consists of primary and secondary students. This program was focused on bridging the digital divide sustainably through training and cost control.

Considering Issues

There are several issues to consider when choosing a location to focus on and selecting a team of individuals for spreading educational technology into developing countries. Quite often locations are brought to us; usually this comes by way of colleagues, family, or friends. As natural educators, we tend to keep an eye out for educational opportunities. When opportunities arise, they come in several forms: Sometimes countries are recommended; other times it is a state, district, or island within a country or even a specific school. While this helps us to narrow down our project area, there are major issues that should be identified, considered, and addressed before moving forward. With the Abaco project, the location was recommended to us by a colleague. (We already had a focus we wanted to address but were looking at two other locations in Ecuador or Mexico).

The first issue, which is often the most limiting, is language barriers. Language barriers make disseminating the information more difficult, although not impossible. Identifying the language barrier up front will help to tailor the project and planning. Language issues must be addressed in the planning phase of the project to make sure there is success. In deciding on Abaco versus Ecuador or Mexico, the language barrier did play a role. If we chose one of the Spanish-speaking countries, we would have needed some Spanish-speaking group members. We would also have to spend time preparing students on language basics. In addition to changing the makeup of the group members, it could affect the budget of a project team if it is necessary to involve translators for the group. If the location has not already been chosen, language barriers could be eliminated or reduced by choosing a location of which the leader of the project has expert knowledge.

Social issues are the second problem that can arise. When working with locations in developing countries, you will often quickly notice that the social issues for that country are different than what you may be accustomed to. Many issues need to be identified and considered before traveling with the team to these countries, including issues related to the economy, social organization, gender roles and inequality, education and public schools, life course, common occupations, environment, and safety. Knowledge of these issues will help you develop an approach to the plan you are attempting to implement; many times, plans will need to be adjusted due to ongoing social issues of the developing country. These adjustments could be slight revisions or drastic overhauls depending on the issue that arises.

It is also important to prepare team members for the social norms of the area so that they can be successful. In determining a location, we evaluated all of the social issues, placing a special emphasis on safety for our students. Once we decided on Abaco, we spent a significant amount of time preparing the students for Abaco and the issues that might arise.

Government and politics is the third issue that will affect the plan, especially when dealing with education, since it is often controlled by government. If the desire is to work in a public school, research should be done on how much control is exercised by the government, what groups can and cannot do, and what resources the school has. The alternative to working with public schools is to work with private schools or organizations, in which case the government control issues are minimized and potential politics do not arise. In our research of Abaco, we evaluated multiple schools, both public and private, and, due to governmental timing restrictions and other political issues, we chose to work with a private school.

The fourth issue to consider is room and board. Many developing countries and areas that we would choose to work in are very rural. Organizers will find that there are not many locations that can house individuals or groups in the chosen locations. Room and board may be difficult and adds a layer of complexity to the project. Transportation should also be a consideration for the project. Room and board and transportation affect the budget of the project as well as the feasibility of the project. In Abaco, there were limited affordable locations for a group of students. We had to decide on a close-enough location to the chosen school for our students to walk daily. Every project will have its own concerns when it relates to room, board, and transportation.

Needs of the school or organization is the final issue to consider in identifying the specific project focus and plan. The school or organization will have specific identified needs, and, of course, there will be needs that your research of the school or organization discloses. Often the needs of the school or organization that you find in your research are indicators of a greater need that they may not have the experience to identify. When evaluating the school, we learned that there was a long list of needs, the majority of which were related to technology. There were peripherals and accessories that, if used appropriately, would add to our original desire of integrating educational technology into developing countries.

Identifying a Focus

After evaluating the language barriers, social issues, governmental and political issues, housing and transportation issues, and needs of the school or organization, there is sufficient information to narrow the focus in educational technology. The idea is to set up a sustainable practice in the school or organization that will enhance the students' education. Through the evaluation of the issues, there will be recurring themes that emerge that will be the most impactful for the organization and the area. When identifying a focus, the organization or school should partner with your group. To ensure that this plan will be sustainable, the organization needs to take an active role in determining the outcomes of the project so its members will be able to continue once the group is gone. The initial focus should be broad enough that specific outcomes could be adjusted but narrow enough that the group can achieve the desired outcomes.

In the focus identification for Abaco, we worked with the school administrators to come up with initial goals. These outcomes centered on the needs of the organization, sustainability, and the skill levels of the students. A few of the outcomes were:

- Ensure the school has working technology to enhance the education provided.

- Ensure faculty in the school has the skills and understanding of how technology can be used in education.

- Ensure the school has individuals that can maintain the technology on campus.

As part of the focus identification for Abaco, there was a scouting, or discovery, trip to help explore the issues. This type of trip is often beneficial in developing a plan for the approach and clearly identifying the issues previously mentioned.

Developing the Plan

The plan for Abaco developed over a period of 6 months. The initial scouting visit occurred in June 2009, and the actual project visit occurred in December 2009. Once the issues were considered and the outcomes developed, the plan could start to take shape. At the forefront of all of our decisions was sustainability. For our projest to be sustainable in Abaco, we would need to keep costs low and focus on training. The training needed to happen with the administration, faculty, and students of the school. The first major set of choices was what technologies to utilize in accomplishing the outcomes. At a minimum, the school needed working computers. We know from James Kulik's meta-analysis research that students with computer-based instruction learn more in less time, develop a more positive attitude toward their classes, and, on average, score higher on tests.[1] Technology decisions were determined based on the availability and accessibility of Windows-based laptops. The school visited disclosed that it received regular donations of laptops but was unable to maintain them.

Laptops alone would not enhance the quality of education provided. Tools for teaching with the technology needed to be provided. In all technology choices, we needed to have a low learning curve and low costs and to ensure it was relevant. Teaching tools come in many forms; the types of tools we chose to focus on were software and projection equipment. The choices of software were limitless, and we needed to narrow this to easy, affordable, and appropriate tools. In addition to providing the tools, we needed to demonstrate and educate the faculty on how to integrate technology into teaching effectively.

For the school to be able to sustain the tools we brought, the project needed to focus considerably on training. There were three approaches to training that needed to occur:

1. Training faculty, including software training, basic technology training, and integrating technology into the course

2. Training students, including computer usage (Figure 8.1), computer repair (Figure 8.2), and computer maintenance

3. Training staff, including inventory methods, technology deployment, and donation requests

Figure 8.1   College students oversee the use of laptops in the Abaco
school

We needed to make sure the effects of the group's visit would not
stop once the group departed. Therefore, we had to give the school tools
to maintain and develop the teaching environment we introduced well
into the future.

Implementing the Plan

The implementation of this plan required a significant amount of
preparation, starting with logistics, which included housing, scheduling
travel and on-site training, shipping of equipment, and project team
training. The on-site logistics for room and board and travel were all
restricted by budget and the school schedule. The budget of the trip
was small enough to limit transportation on the island and require a few
self-pay rooms. The project team was predetermined based on college
enrollment. The students assigned to this course showed interest in the
course but were not hand-selected by the leader of the project. One
challenge in the process was the shipping of any technology we would
be sending to the school. We chose to bring part of the equipment
and ship the other part, which took over a month to be received. This
seems to be a common issue in several developing countries. It relates

Figure 8.2   Abaco students are taught how to fix a computer

to infrastructure issues and could potentially be uncovered when doing the initial research.

In addition to the basic logistics, the team needed to be trained on the skills that they would be passing on to the individuals of the school. Once they were trained, they needed time to plan how they would train the individuals at the school. The preparation of the students was done in two parts. At the college, we attached a full-semester course to the project that taught students about the digital divide. This provided them with a deep understanding of the issues that arise from the divide and how some individuals may approach working to bridge the divide domestically. The students were also prepared for the social issues they would experience in Abaco. The second part of the training dealt with specific planning for the on-site visit. The team was split into four groups. Two groups focused on technology in education and how technology could be used in the classroom. Another group focused on video development with a specialized set of students, and the final group focused on maintenance of the equipment and training select students and staff at the school. Each group was self-selected and determined about halfway through the semester. Once the groups were determined, the groups went through specialized training to ensure they had the necessary skills to bring to Abaco.

In addition to training, the students built lesson plans for the on-site project (see Figure 8.3 for an example). The lesson plans focused on teaching the students in Abaco to use technology tools. The plans left time for the college students to work with the faculty later in the day to train them on how to replicate and/or utilize the same tools in the classroom in their teaching. While the students developed these plans, they also compiled a list of software they would need for the visit. The limitations on choices were the same as before: easy, affordable, and applicable. We purchased the software and donated the software suites to the school to continue use. In addition to software purchases, any peripherals needed, such as headphones, repair toolsets, CDs, mice, and so on, were purchased and donated to the school. The money for these donations came from fundraising by the college students prior to the trip.

Once the preparation was complete, the on-site visit took place, with some time incorporated for exploration of the community. This was to help the students learn more about the culture and allow them to decompress from teaching. The schedule was carefully planned to balance the

Daily Lesson Plans - Wednesday		
Subjects & Objectives	**Materials/Tools**	**Procedures**
8:30 – 9:15	Prep Time	
9:15–10:15 Training Session 1	Make sure they know how to install software onto a computer. Ex. Antivirus software. Also, how to identify the symptoms of a problem.	Computer Repair Tool kit Working Computer Broken Computer Different CDs they may want to install, ex. Games Evaluating and Solving CD given to us by IT	Instruct them on installing software. Where to save it, icon use, and what it does and why it is needed. Teach them the different symptoms that reflect a problem.
10:30–11:15 Training Session 2	Make sure they know how to fix computers hardware, replace parts, and use the software to repair operating issues.	Computer Repair Tool kit Working Computer Broken Computer Additional parts inside of a computer, like a hard drive or disk drive Evaluating and Solving CD given to us by IT	Show them how to open computers and laptops, take out hardware and replace it. Teach them to recognize the different hardware parts. Also, show them when replacing internal hardware parts would be necessary.
11:30–12:15 Training Session 3	Make sure they know how to set up projectors and audio video equipment, and how to replace projector bulb and clean filter. Also, how to perform a power cycle.	Computer Repair Tool kit Working Computer Broken Computer Evaluating and Solving CD given to us by IT Audio video equipment and Projector	Show them how to set up projectors and audio video equipment and how to replace a projector bulb and clean its filter. Also how to perform power cycle.
1:00 – 2:45	Fix/Repair/A/V in front of our students.	

Figure 8.3 Typical lesson plan

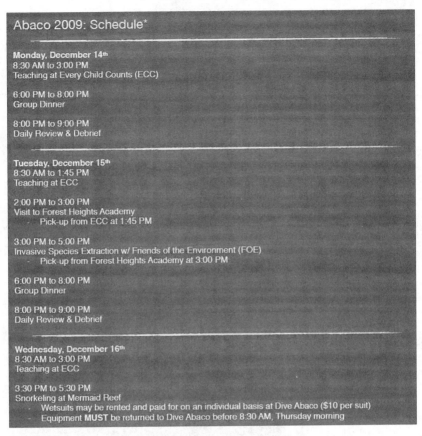

Figure 8.4   Schedule of project and cultural events

project with cultural exploration. A sample of the schedule can be seen in Figure 8.4.

Each day there was a debrief with the project team that allowed for issues to be disclosed and the day's events to be processed. In the debrief, we would attempt to solve any pressing issues before the next day's work. In addition to the debrief, the students completed blog posts (Figure 8.5).

Accomplishments

The project team accomplished several tasks in Abaco. If we look back to the intended outcomes of the project, the majority of the tasks led to accomplishing the outcomes. Figure 8.6 groups the team's tasks into the desired outcomes.

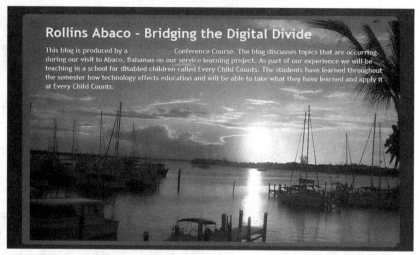

Figure 8.5   The project blog

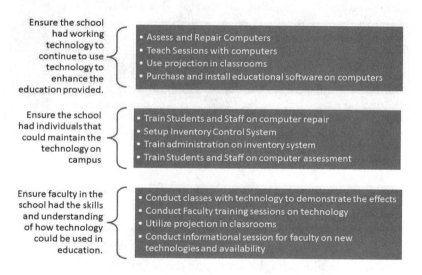

Figure 8.6   Breakdown of tasks and the desired outcomes

By time we left, the school in Abaco had a complete set of working laptops, a group of students and a staff member with basic computer troubleshooting skills, and a system for inventorying and distributing the laptops to the classrooms. The faculty of the school received basic training on using technology in the classroom and was provided projection equipment to utilize some of these tools. The final accomplishment did not fall directly within the outcomes, but it was a direct response to a request of the school. A group of the students in Abaco, along with one faculty member, were taught the basics of video production, and the students collaborated on a video project for the school.

Conclusion

There were several factors that led to the Abaco project being successful. The key factors were the focus on sustainability, the preparation of the group, and the ongoing relationship. The trip to Abaco focused on achieving sustainability through training and cost control. As with any project, there were hundreds of methods the group could have used. As mentioned earlier in this chapter, it is very important to narrow the focus in order to make it accomplishable. This is what we did. It was very difficult to keep such a focus, but it allowed us to make choices in how to proceed with the project and be successful. All of the decisions on tasks and plans were made with sustainability and outcomes in the forefront.

The preparation of the project was the next key element contributing to the success of the project. Quite often in educational technology, there is a specific set of skills individuals need to accomplish the desired outcomes. It may be impossible to find a team that already has all of the skills needed. There needs to be enough preparation time built in to ensure the team can implement and train the individuals in the school. We struggled with this during the pre-trip phase. Difficulty in coordinating schedules resulted in less training than preferred. We also struggled with limiting the number of tasks to undertake while on-site. The school had a number of tasks that they expressed a desire to complete, but we had to choose ones that would result in meeting the original goals. We needed to make sure we could prepare appropriately for the on-site visit.

Finally, a sustainable project is one in which the effects continue for an extended period of time. This project, similar to others, needed follow-up. The group was able to set up basic training, but this would only take the school so far. As part of the ongoing support, we set up methods for continuing communication with the school. Since the original trip in 2009, there have been two other trips, and the partnership is set to continue annually. The partnership developed between our college and the school in Abaco continues to flourish and has helped this school in Abaco progress well into the future.

Endnote

1. James A. Kulik, "Meta-Analytic Studies on Findings on Computer-Based Instruction," in *Technology Assessment in Education and Training*, ed. Eva L. Baker and Harold F. O'Neil, Jr. (Hillsdale, NJ: Lawrence Erlbaum, 1994), 9–34.

CHAPTER 9

Design Education for Social Innovation Supported by Technology: The Safe Agua Case Study

Mariana Amatullo, Dan Gottlieb, and Penny Herscovitch

Portions of this chapter were first published in the paper by Mariana Amatullo and Penny Herscovitch, entitled "Perspectives About Design Education for Social Innovation: The Safe Agua Case Study," in November 2012, by the Cumulus International Association of Universities and Colleges of Art, Design and Media, for the Projecting Design 2012 Conference.

Nothing has to be or to remain as it is or as it appears to be; there are no limits to the conceivable.

—Horst W.J. Rittel (1987)

There is a revolutionary transformation underway in the design field at large as it continues to expand its meaning, shape human experience, and influence other knowledge domains and contemporary culture in a broader scope than at any time in the past. In their most essential roles, designers today deal with concrete and objective results whose consequences affect us all, shaping the form, function, and symbols of our world: from the visualization, ideation, and planning of images, products, and services to the strategic conceptualization of systems and environments (Buchanan 1994).

Increasingly, designers are also called upon as translators and synthesizers of a class of societal challenges that are ill-defined, ill-structured, and "wicked" (Rittel and Webber 1973).

Parallel to the shift in the field of design, the extraordinary expansion of technologies available to design students has afforded a new set of tools to address these challenges: from 3D printing and rapid prototyping to quickly iterate functioning design prototypes to point-to-point videoconferencing and online translators to facilitate collaboration with partners across borders and cultures.

This chapter offers an in-depth overview and articulation of the evolving pedagogical methods and design outcomes of Safe Agua, a flagship initiative facilitated by Designmatters at Art Center College of Design. Safe Agua focuses on meeting the challenges of safe water access for populations of urban slum dwellers in Chile and Peru and is the result of an ongoing partnership between Designmatters and the Innovation Center of the NGO Techo (now known as Socialab), headquartered in Santiago, Chile.[1]

In the context of the analysis of the Safe Agua case study, this chapter also poses opportunities and challenges inherent in integrating new technology, social media, and rapid prototyping to support new pedagogical models for design education that aspire to social innovation outcomes.

A Journey Beyond the Studio: An Overview of Safe Agua Chile and Peru

Clean water is essential to life; lack of access to it results in poor health and economic hardship. In our interlinked economies, access to safe water in one community quickly becomes a global issue that affects us all. Experts forecast that, by 2030, demand for water will be 50 percent higher than it is today, and withdrawals could exceed natural renewal by 60 percent, making water scarcity an even more dire reality for a third of the world's population (2030 Water Resources Group 2009).

Over two academic terms in 2009, Designmatters at the Art Center College of Design partnered with the Innovation Center of the Chilean organization Un Techo para mi País, which has offices in 19 countries throughout Latin America, to sponsor studios in which undergraduate students traveled to Chilean slums and worked directly with residents to envision, design, and test solutions addressing the lack of safe running water. For residents of Fundo San Jose, in the outskirts of Santiago, Chile, the team, calling itself Safe Agua Chile, generated six solutions involving the use, storage, and transportation of water.

In 2011, the same staff and faculty leadership team extended the Safe Agua project to a Peruvian slum with key support of a Sustainable Vision grant from the National Collegiate Inventors and Innovators Alliance (NCIIA).[2] The Safe Agua Peru team sought opportunities for water system innovations, capitalizing on the field research and outcomes of the Chilean project. The Peru project included a new studio class of students from the undergraduate Environmental, Product, and Graphic Design departments in an advanced-level transdisciplinary studio hosted by the Environmental Design Department at Art Center. A Graduate Broadcast Cinema student was also enrolled in the project to produce a documentary about the collaboration.[3]

The project began in September 2011, with a 10-day intensive field research trip to Cerro Verde, a community perched high in the hills of Lima with no access to basic services. This community was identified with the team of Un Techo para mi País Peru, in Lima, and the Techo Innovation team based in Santiago (Figure 9.1). Driven by field research and continuous dialogue with a cluster of approximately 20 families from Cerro who agreed to participate in the studio, teams designed a series of proposed products and systems to address water scarcity. They created full-scale working prototypes, which were tested in Peru, then further iterated upon and refined based on several loops of feedback with the community of end users and partners in Peru.

Six Proposals

By the end of the studio's full academic term in December 2011 (16 weeks into the project), and based on lessons learned from testing and

Figure 9.1   Participatory field research in the Community of Cerro Verde, Lima, Peru

user feedback, the Safe Agua Peru teams developed designs that aspired to enhance benefits and functionality for users (including health benefits, convenience, and water savings; user experience; educational value; and appeal to children) while targeting affordability and potential for local manufacturing and effective distribution. The following six working prototypes were proposed.

GiraDora, designed by Ji A You and Alex Cabunoc, is an innovative concept for a human-powered combined washer and spin dryer for families earning $4 to $10 (U.S.) a day (Figure 9.2). Currently, hand-washing clothes is a time-intensive chore that takes up to 20 hours a week, consumes much of families' scarce water, and can lead to health risks. GiraDora reduces the time to hand-wash a load of laundry from 1 hour to 3 or 5 minutes, uses one-third less water, and improves the experience of hand-washing clothes for women living without access to running water. The user sits on the drum-like appliance and pumps the pedal with her foot to agitate, clean, rinse, and spin-dry clothes. Local assembly and an innovative business plan with three revenue streams for micro-entrepreneurs provide supplemental income. At a price point currently under $40 (U.S.), GiraDora's comfortable and ergonomic operation significantly increases productivity, reduces health risks, instills dignity, and affords opportunities to begin breaking the poverty cycle.

Balde a Balde (Spanish for "Bucket to Bucket"), designed by Kim Chow, is a portable faucet that delivers a flow of water from any container (Figure 9.3). Lack of running water is associated with a decreased incidence of hand-washing and an increased risk of diarrhea—one of the leading causes of death for children under five globally (UNICEF/

Figure 9.2   GiraDora clothes-washer/spin-dryer prototype

Figure 9.3 *Balde a Balde* prototype testing

World Health Organization [WHO] 2009). *Balde a Balde* makes the convenience and health benefits of running water available to the two out of 10 urban dwellers and seven out of 10 rural dwellers who lack access to piped water connections (WHO/UNICEF 2010). Unlike other hand-washing interventions, *Balde a Balde* does not just address clean hands, but also optimizes the full range of water-related tasks performed in the home. *Balde a Balde* provides running water wherever it is needed: A universal clip attaches the portable faucet to any existing container; a squeeze of the siphon pump initiates a continuous flow of water; tapping the spout instantly turns on and off the water; and twisting the valve regulates the volume of water.

VitAmigos, conceived by Cora Neil and Thomas Kong, proposes a new, fun, playful, and interactive experience for mothers and children that combines water purification and nutrition in a tasty beverage (Figure 9.4). For families living without access to safe water, VitAmigos seeks to reduce waterborne illness and improve children's health for less than the cost of a soda. VitAmigos is not just a vitamin-enriched water; it also provides an educational experience for children. Comprised of a playful and durable clear pitcher and time-release tablets, it works in phases: First, the tablet purifies the nonpotable water; it then dissolves to create a vitamin-rich beverage, with a fun color that indicates it is safe and ready to drink.

Clean+Smart, designed by Mariana Prieto and Alexandra Yee, uses small detergent packages as the vehicle to deliver ADI (from the Spanish for build [*arma*], discover [*descubre*], and inspire [*inspira*]) Educational Toys to children living in extreme poverty. Detergent is a commodity that is purchased very frequently in small packages throughout slums

Figure 9.4   VitAmigos water purification and vitamin tablet by Cora
Neil and Thomas Kong

in Latin America. Clean+Smart gives families with children a low-cost
opportunity to collect high-quality toys that can support their children's
development in the home (Figure 9.5).

Caja del Tesoro, designed by Seth Weissman and Viirj Kan, is an
analog vending machine and microbusiness initiative that gives women
living at the base of the pyramid (BoP) the skills and tools necessary
to help them earn their way out of poverty. The stand-alone storefront
adjusts to vend a range of products, providing a convenient, safe, and
accessible place for slum communities to purchase necessities any time
of the day or night. The concept includes an entrepreneurship program

Figure 9.5   Clean+Smart

to empower women to generate income for their families, while providing value for their communities (Figure 9.6).

Soap Buddy, designed by Carlos Vides, is a soap-dispensing bracelet for kids that promotes hand-washing by making soap more accessible and fun. Hand-washing is critical to preventing diarrheal illnesses and can reduce many water-related deaths two times more than drinking clean water alone can (Charity: Water 2013). Soap Buddy makes hand-washing fun by extruding paste soap (common in developing countries) though the bracelet's faceplate. The interchangeable faceplates become animated when the soap is extruded: Spiderman shoots out a soap web, Hello Kitty's whiskers grow, or roses grow from a stem.

Figure 9.6 Caja del Tesoro

Next Steps

The student teams that have moved forward into a new phase of iteration and development all have in common the fact that their designs resonated strongly with the families they engaged with and the project's partner; these teams have also demonstrated entrepreneurship intent in wanting to see their patent-pending prototypes advance to a new phase of development, beyond the studio course, that includes a second round of pilot testing and impact assessment (under way at this writing) in slum communities in Santiago, Chile, closer to the Innovation Center's Chilean headquarters. The *Balde a Balde* and GiraDora teams are currently working with a team of faculty and students from the Society and Business Lab at the University of Southern California Marshall School of Business; Clean+Smart is pursuing commercialization strategies, and VitAmigos is collaborating in turn with chemistry experts from the California Institute of Technology to research water purification technologies appropriate to their design system.

A further stage of testing in Latin America was done in 2013, based on the local support and social enterprise network of the Techo Innovation team, and with the support of two NCIIA E-Team grants for *Balde a Balde* and GiraDora. This is key support, as NCIIA makes awards to multidisciplinary teams of students and faculty to bring to market promising innovations. These two E-Teams have joined forces to launch Blue Barrel Concepts LLC, a social enterprise to develop and launch high-impact products in partnership with international manufacturers.

The Design Challenge and Framework Criteria

The Safe Agua studio posed the following design challenge: "How can we work with families living in Peru's *asentamientos* (slums) to design and develop solutions, products, and services for using, obtaining, containing, and carrying water in order to help break the cycle of poverty?" This challenge was framed with a market-based approach, guided by the social entrepreneurship thought leader C. K. Prahalad:

> If we stop thinking of the poor as victims ... and start recognizing them as resilient and creative entrepreneurs and value-conscious consumers, a whole new world of opportunity can open up. Four billion poor can be the engine of

the next round of global trade and prosperity. They can be a source of innovations. (2006, 1)

Design criteria were established through the lens of social entrepreneur Paul Polak's book *Out of Poverty* (2009) as well as Polak's teachings at an NCIIA workshop attended by the Product Design lead faculty of the project. Polak's charge was to "make sure your approach has positive measurable impacts that can be brought to scale [and] make sure it can reach at least a million people and make their lives measurably better" (2009, 14), along with joint goals established by the Designmatters team and the innovation team at Techo. Key drivers were outlined as follows:

- Scalable, sustainable solutions with potential for real-world implementation

- Radically affordable products and services for Base of the Pyramid (BoP)

- Solutions that address specific problems, with both quantitative impacts (illness reduction, water conservation, increased time for self-improvement, opportunities to generate income) and qualitative impacts (sense of dignity)

- Solutions at the scales of products for individuals and households, and products, spaces, and services for a small group of families (which can in turn benefit a larger group), along with services for many communities

To guide students in integrating these criteria from the outset, the teaching team expanded beyond the Environmental and Product Design faculty who previously led Safe Agua Chile. To achieve deeper field research results, an ethnography instructor collaborated on framing the field research methodologies and co-led the field research trip. During the term, the instructor continued to lead a corequisite ethnography seminar embedded in the design studio to articulate problems, construct compelling stories, and contextualize the studio work with discussion and readings on poverty, slums, the role of water, social innovation, and BoP entrepreneurship case studies. Additionally, the class integrated workshops, lectures, and consultation by a business teaching assistant, a University of

Southern California Marshall School of Business MBA candidate and Society and Business Lab fellow.[4] As the projects progressed, the business teaching assistant guided teams through the process of framing business models, using tools from *Business Model Generation: A Handbook for Visionaries, Game Changers, and Challengers* (Osterwalder and Pigneur 2010).

Field Research and Designerly Ways of Knowing

The following section provides an overview of the key design research strategies and exercises for immersive learning that were used in the Safe Agua studio. Many of the methods articulated were greatly informed by methods deployed in the previously led studio, Safe Agua Chile (Amatullo, Becerra, and Montgomery 2010; Herscovitch et al. 2010), and others were co-developed with the design research ethnography expertise referenced earlier. This integration of academic and studio instruction is an important hallmark of all transdisciplinary studios at Art Center and proves increasingly essential to support the accelerated pace of learning that projects such as Safe Agua demand.

Exercise in Empathy: A Day Without Taps

Successful design is rooted in empathy. To prepare for the research trip, "A Day Without Taps" was developed as an effective exercise that visualized a measure of constraints the students would encounter in the field. Each student and faculty member purchased five gallons of water to use for all daily activities for one day, and carried it home on foot, bike, or public transit; they also boiled their drinking water. The goal of this exercise was to become conscious of how we use water in our daily lives and to dedicate one day to understanding how our lives would be different without convenient access to water. This exercise built empathy with the families the team worked with in Cerro Verde, who purchase nonpotable water from a delivery truck (at 14 times the cost per gallon that Lima's middle-class city dwellers pay), store the water in barrels along the dirt road, and hand-carry water up hundreds of hillside steps.

The Field Research Trip

Development of Safe Agua Peru began with a 10-day intensive research trip to Cerro Verde. Two core families hosted each research team of two students, with a total of 20 in-depth interviews conducted collectively.

During the visits, the teams participated in daily activities and helped with daily chores, gathered quantitative data, discussed people's aspirations and life stories, and bonded with families. At Techo's office in Peru, to prepare for working with families in the field, the teams conducted a role-playing exercise to practice interviews with a translator, developed interview questions, and met with Cerro Verde's two community leaders.

Methodologies

A set of methodology cards (Figure 9.7), which built on those developed for Safe Agua Chile, guided ethnographic research methods to collect both quantitative and qualitative information. The cards were intended as a generative starting point for gaining insights into another culture, rather than a prescriptive method. They outlined seven areas of focus, three specifically related to water and four broad topics beyond water.

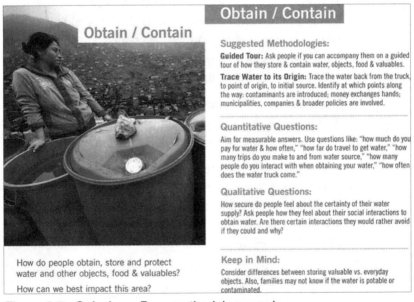

Figure 9.7   Safe Agua Peru methodology cards

The cards' design was based in part on the collective experience of the faculty as well as inspiration from IDEO's method cards (Stout 2003) to help overcome language and cultural barriers, with methodologies targeted to each topic:

- *Day in the life:* Suggested methodologies included giving inexpensive digital cameras to the family members to keep and narrate a photo journal of their daily life. Quantitative questions included budgets, earnings, and time spent on work, family, and chores.

- *Aspirations/limitations:* Methodologies included card sorting. Qualitative questions included what steps people are taking to achieve their dreams and goals and what larger structures (policy, class issues) might prevent people from achieving them. The findings from this card—that people's highest aspirations were for their children to succeed as well as to own their own house and earn more income—drove the larger missions of each team well beyond water.

- *Materials and making:* Methodologies included gathering existing individual and local skill sets and innovative solutions that people have created. Questions included asking people what objects are missing from their lives in order for them to perform daily tasks.

- *Maps and networks:* Methodologies included drawing an ideal home layout, mapping paths people take to perform water-related actions.

- *Obtain/contain water*: Methodologies included guided tours and tracing water back to its source, identifying at which points contaminants are introduced, money exchanges hands, and municipalities, companies, and broader policies are involved.

- *Carry/move:* Methodologies included flow analysis and storyboarding the path that water takes. Key questions included "How can minimizing carrying and moving water impact people's health and afford free time for self-improvement activities?"

- *Use/reuse of water:* Methodologies included participating in daily water-related chores (laundry, dishes, cooking, cleaning home, etc.), then drawing a

step-by-step action map of each routine and asking at
what point along each action map design
opportunities lie.

Initial Problem Identification and "What Ifs"

In a first-stage post-field immersion, teams mapped their insights, visualizing the various threads of immediate findings with posted notes that were organized under the meta-questions "What's the problem?" and "What if ...?" The teams collectively ranked the most pressing problems and returned to the field to ask families to rank their highest priorities, posing what-if scenarios and solutions together. While students often came up with "blue sky," abstract solutions, families tended to gravitate toward pragmatic ideas with concrete steps addressing each problem. To understand the broader framework of each key problem, teams created maps that traced back to root causes and sketched forward potential implications. A presentation on BoP trends, aspirations, and inclusive business models by Lima-based staff from the Netherlands-founded nonprofit organization Stichting Nederlandse Vrijwilligers (SNV), which works worldwide to develop best practices for sustainable development,[5] was key to contextualizing the field research. The SNV Peru-based team of researchers added important data and guidance that was informed by years of research working with BoP communities in Peru.

Design for Social Innovation: The Pedagogical Journey

The Safe Agua studio (Figure 9.8) stands apart from many other studio classes typically present in the Art Center undergraduate curriculum in that students are not assigned a design brief per se but are instead offered an ill-defined "wicked" problem to wrestle with and a specific context that grounds it. Faculty members mentor the students and guide them through an open-ended process of "opportunity definition" that occurs in the field with end users and partners. In this sense, the design research methodologies that informed the Safe Agua studio, as with most Designmatters collaborations, follow a long lineage of participatory design research modes of engagement. Participatory design is widely recognized today as offering important advantages to a design team that can draw upon the tacit knowledge of users to identify issues and solutions that may otherwise elude them (Press and Cooper 2003). In designing for a specific group or context, users may also gain a sense of

Figure 9.8   The Safe Agua Peru studio/visual map

ownership about the design that can lead to more successful outcomes. In this context, the Safe Agua project approach epitomizes a project that engages designers, principles of design thinking, co-creation, and participatory design to place people at the center of the design exploration and process—beyond reducing them to "end users" (Buchanan 2001).

The participatory arc of the project continued well past the field research immersion. The teams took initial findings and began to analyze and synthesize the data to define key problems. To ensure that framing occurred within a dialectic process that asked questions of relevance and, most importantly, would maximize the chances for proposed products that the families would be eager and able to purchase, the teams sought opportunities that connected with both observed behavioral patterns and consumption patterns (i.e., cost, time, and health). Teams also identified market opportunities with the potential of broad-based impact (the ideal target scale of beneficiaries was held at the 1 million-plus mark).

Beyond the Field: Transnational Co-Creation Supported by Communication Technology

In response to a critique from Techo that Safe Agua Chile did not fully achieve a true process of co-creation, the team sought more meaningful connections between students and families throughout the Peru project, beyond the field research stage. Key technologies utilized to extend the dialogue between students in California, the NGO team in Santiago and Chile, and families in Peru included regular team consultations via online video conferencing (Skype) and social networking (Facebook) with the Techo team headquartered in Santiago, Chile; and conversations with the families in the study via Nextel international "walkie-talkie" phones, which Techo provided at no cost to the community leaders. These tactics used for ongoing dialogue led to co-created "opportunity definition spaces." In the next step of validating initial design directions, design teams emailed co-creation documents (including a clear problem statement and storyboard, drawings of three potential solutions, and specific questions) for the Techo team to use as a tool to elicit feedback from Cerro Verde families. These regular feedback loops during prototype development continued to dictate the direction of the design development.

Based on lessons learned from Safe Agua Peru, in future projects we will seek to implement technologies to strengthen direct communication between student teams in California and stakeholders abroad. As affordable smartphones and mobile technologies become more accessible in emerging markets, we propose incorporating social media and custom apps to facilitate new modes of research and co-creation at a distance, and to help bridge the gap between designer and end user. We see strong potential for communication technologies to connect voices, opinions, and feedback from individuals living in poverty with teams seeking solutions to overcome water poverty, ensuring a great deal of interaction between the design team and the end users.

Iterative Prototyping and Digital Fabrication Technologies

The objective of the prototyping phase was to develop design solutions that respond to the opportunities identified, via a process of brainstorming and sketching, storytelling, and building iterative prototypes. Inspired by Polak, this quick prototyping focused on the premise of developing "tools for empowerment" rather than dead-end objects (Polak 2011).

A "Thinking Through Making" exercise transitioned from the problem definition phase to the iterative prototyping phase. The goal of the exercise was to begin to make rough "proof-of-concept" prototypes to ideate off the page, through making and hands-on exploration.

The Art Center 3D Lab's rapid prototyping technologies, including laser-cutting, 3D printing parts designed in Solidworks using a Z-Corp 3D plaster printer, and a Fused Deposition Modeling (FDM) 3D printer into ABS plastic, were instrumental in creating iterative, functioning prototypes that worked with water. Students integrated custom 3D-printed and laser-cut parts with off-the-shelf, mass-produced parts to rapidly create, test, and improve prototypes. For example, *Balde a Balde* leveraged this resourceful approach, combining a 3D-printed faucet head (designed to be injection molded for mass production) with an off-the-shelf bulb pump and hosing, yielding a radically affordable portable faucet that optimizes both effectiveness and manufacturing cost.

Field Testing Prototypes

After initial rounds of design exploration, all teams created working prototypes for midterm presentations. Two weeks after midterm, two student representatives—a bilingual Product Design student and the graduate broadcast media documentary filmmaker—brought all the prototypes to Peru for field-testing. We timed the field-testing to give students a meaningful deadline to make a big leap forward after midterm, then receive feedback with 4 to 5 weeks to implement into final designs. With key support from Techo, the students tested the teams' working prototypes in Cerro Verde with five families for 4 days and left robust prototypes with families for longer-term trials. The student researchers also conducted focus group discussions and surveys with large groups of women, and visited a local school. The families in Peru responded to these working prototypes, shared their own ideas, and showed us exactly what they valued and what they wanted to change. Back in California, the research team downloaded their field notes and shared documentary footage of interviews and product testing with each team.

This direct interaction with end users afforded insights that drove the designs, and, in some cases, fundamentally shifted a team's design direction. For instance, Team GiraDora sent two separate prototypes: a plunger–like washing device and a salad-spinner inspired dryer. Immediately, the women of Cerro Verde identified the highest value in combining the washing and drying prototypes into a single device, which dictated the team's final design direction.

Lessons learned from Safe Agua Chile drove the decision to allocate limited resources to a second field trip—which had not occurred for Safe Agua Chile. Safe Agua Peru instead allowed for feedback during field-testing at a critical juncture of the studio (midterm), and having access to this feedback that the two students assigned to go back to Peru brought back yielded a unique educational experience for the entire class. The salient values proposed by the final designs (i.e., benefits to users, including health, convenience, water savings, user experience, and educational value) are a direct outcome of those closer interactions between the design team and the families.

Beyond the Initial Studio: Project Development Toward Pilot Testing

In the spring of 2012, a new course in the Art Center curriculum, the Designmatters Development Seminar, was created to ensure that faculty mentorship and resources would be available to support the student teams who had expressed interest in continuing development on their design innovations. Safe Agua Peru's VitAmigos, *Balde a Balde*, GiraDora, and Clean+Smart teams have developed their prototypes and incubated business strategies. The teams have explored human-centered/participatory design research methodologies and user testing; employed rapid prototyping, collaboration, and innovation techniques; practiced project management and leadership; and gained a broad exposure to resources for developing implementation scenarios through access to outside partnerships and grants that will carry these innovations to a new amplified pilot testing phase in 2013. It is anticipated that in this phase, the teams will have to conquer a number of challenges inherent in pilot rollout of social innovation proposals including: 1) the identification of a local social entrepreneur or implementation partner that may have the potential to accelerate the rate of testing and finalization for the projects to move forward to an amplified scale of pilot rollout; and 2) the design of appropriate distribution pathways and commercialization strategies for each project.

Teams have pitched to potential investors and partners in Latin America via point-to-point videoconferencing. Online competitions, video-sharing sites, and media have led to funding and publicity. Social media continues to serve as a valuable platform to communicate the results of Safe Agua and to connect with partners and potential customers, as the student teams move toward real-world implementation.

Conclusion

The Safe Agua Peru case study presents an example of an immersive design education model for social innovation that required a rigorous process of collaboration with local partners and end users, field research, methodologies of co-creation, iterative prototyping, field-testing and evaluation, and a critical base of knowledge imparted to the student team outside design. As a continuation of the Safe Agua Chile project and reliant on a strong partnership with the Techo Innovation Center and the same staff/faculty leadership team at Art Center, Safe Agua Peru also demonstrates the value of taking a "building block" incremental approach. With Safe Agua Peru, strong outcomes for the students involved and social impact on the communities are linked to increasing knowledge gained over time, iteration, and collaboration.

New modes of collaboration, connectivity, and ongoing communication facilitated by technology are reshaping the design process. As the availability of smartphones and internet connectivity grows in underserved communities, we see extraordinary potential for the voices and opinions of individuals living in poverty to help shape the next set of tools for overcoming water poverty.

Social innovation applies to a broad spectrum of contexts. To design education, it correlates closely with putting in place curricula where students can experience and learn about the real and positive impact the systems, strategies, products, and services they conceive as designers can afford individuals and groups of people who live in highly resource-constrained environments. Projects such as Safe Agua aspire to make a tangible difference by setting forth new pedagogical models that are characterized by their openness to experimentation, a mode of responsible engagement with collaborators, and the adoption and invention of new technologies for collaboration and co-creation. The return on investment for advancing the articulation of design as a key contributor to social innovation at large cannot be overestimated.

Endnotes

1. The authors are indebted to the leadership and vision of Julián Ugarte, founder and director of the Innovation Center of Un Techo para mi País (now known as Socialab) and his team for their ongoing partnership. For more information on Socialab, go to socialab.com.

2. Designmatters at Art Center College of Design is a repeat grantee of the NCIIA, whose mission is to support technology innovation and entrepreneurship in universities and colleges to create experiential learning opportunities for students and successful, socially beneficial businesses. For more information, go to nciia.org.

3. The Art Center's Safe Agua Peru faculty team is composed of Liliana Becerra (Product Design); Penny Herscovitch and Daniel Gottlieb (Environmental Design); Julka Almquist (Humanities and Design Sciences Department); and teaching assistant KC Cho (Product Design). Students are Erik Anderson (Graduate Broadcast Media); Bianca Fuchs (Graphic Design); Viirj Kan, Cora Neil, Carlos Vides, Alexandra Yee, and Ji A You (Environmental Design); and Kimberly Chow, Alex Robert Cabunoc, Thomas Kong, Mariana Prieto, and Seth M. Weissman (Product Design). Department chairs are David Mocarski (Environmental Design) and Karen Hofmann (Product Design). The Designmatters department team includes co-founder and vice president Mariana Amatullo and director Elisa Ruffino.

4. Designmatters partners on an ongoing basis with the team led by Professor Adlai Wertman of the Business and Society Lab at the Marshall School of Business at University of Southern California (USC). The teaching assistant was Tracy L. Dennis, MBA candidate (May 2012) at the Marshall School of Business at USC. The "E-teams" of *Balde a Balde* and GiraDora now include USC MBA candidate Jonathan A. Beckhardt.

5. SNV leads an important initiative focused on water, sanitation, and hygiene in Peru among other regions (snvworld.org/en/sectors/water-sanitation-hygiene). To learn more about SNV, go to snvworld.org.

References

Amatullo, Mariana, Liliana Becerra, and Steven Montgomery. 2010. "Designmatters Case Studies: Design Education Methodologies as a Tool for Social Innovation." Paper presented at NCIIA. nciia.org/sites/default/files/u7/Amatullo.pdf.

Buchanan, Richard. 1994. "Branzi's Dilemma: Design in Contemporary Culture." Keynote address delivered at "Design: Pleasure or Responsibility," University of Art and Design Helsinki.

———. 2001. "Human Dignity and Human Rights: Thoughts on the Principles of Human-Centered Design." *Design Issues* 17(3): 35–39.

Charity: Water. 2013. "Why Water?" www.charitywater.org/whywater.

Herscovitch, Penny, Dan Gottlieb, Liliana Becerra, Mariana Amatullo, and David Morcarski. 2010. "Safe Agua: A Collaboration Between Un Techo para mi País and Art Center College of Design." Paper presented at Cumulus Shanghai Conference. www.designmattersatartcenter.org/wp-content/content/pdf/publications/papers/herscovitch_cumulus_paper.pdf.

Osterwalder, Alexander, and Yves Pigneur. 2010. *Business Model Generation: A Handbook for Visionaries, Game Changers, and Challengers*. Hoboken, NJ: Wiley.

Polak, Paul. 2009. *Out of Poverty: What Works When Traditional Approaches Fail*. San Francisco: Berrett-Koehler Publishers.

———. 2011. "Sustainable Vision Teaching Lab—NCIIA," Lecture conducted from Colorado State University, June 13–17. www.designmattersatartcenter.org/2011/08/03/sustainable-vision-teaching-lab-nciia-colorado-state-university-june-13-17-2011.

Prahalad, C.K. 2006. *The Fortune at the Bottom of the Pyramid: Eradicating Poverty Through Profits.* Upper Saddle River, NJ: Prentice Hall.

Press, Michael, and Rachel Cooper. 2003. *The Design Experience: The Role of Design and Designers in the Twenty-First Century.* Burlington, VT: Ashgate Publishing Limited.

Rittel, Horst W.J. 1987. "The Reasoning of Designers." Speech delivered at the University of California, Berkeley.

Rittel, Horst W.J., and Melvin M. Webber. 1973. "Dilemmas in a General Theory of Planning." *Policy Sciences* 4: 155–169.

Stout, William. 2003. *IDEO Method Cards: 51 Ways to Inspire Design.* Palo Alto, CA: IDEO.

2030 Water Resources Group. 2009. "Charting Our Water Future: Economic Frameworks to Inform Decision-Making." www.mckinsey.com/App_Media/Reports/Water/Charting_Our_Water_Future_Full_Report_001.pdf.

UNICEF/World Health Organization. 2009. *Diarrhea: Why Children Are Still Dying and What Can Be Done.* whqlibdoc.who.int/publications/2009/9789241598415_eng.pdf.

WHO/UNICEF. 2010. *Progress on Sanitation and Drinking Water: 2010 Update.* www.unwater.org/downloads/JMP_report_2010.pdf.

CHAPTER 10

Emerging Technology in the Schools of Rwanda

J. Scott Hewit and Abigail Bragg New

Developing nations are characterized by a pervasively low standard of living, the absence of a strong industrial foundation, and other measures that include life expectancy, level of education, and income relative to developed countries. The rapid growth of technology worldwide, however, has impacted developing nations in ways that may blur the borders between developing and developed nations. As technology facilitates communication and commerce between people from different cultures around the globe, it provides unprecedented access to those in developing nations who are using mobile phones in record numbers. For example, farmers in Niger are using their mobile technology to improve trading profits, while medical services have been enhanced in many African nations as the result of text messaging capabilities.

This chapter focuses on the emergence of technology in Rwanda (in particular, rural Rwanda) and how it is impacting the delivery of learning in primary and secondary schools there. A brief history of the role of education in Rwanda provides a context from which to gain an appreciation for the recent expansion of technology throughout this region. The role of technology in the education of young Rwandans is more fully understood through the lens of what has transpired in this small, densely populated country in the last hundred years, and particularly since the genocide of 1994. The actual emergence of technology in Rwandan schools is described, with particular attention to the work of One Laptop Per Child, a nonprofit organization dedicated to providing laptop computers to students in developing countries. A description of the integration of technology into one poor rural school follows, including specifics leading up to the integration and future aspirations of both local school leaders and teachers at the school.

A Brief History of Education in Rwanda

Schools often serve as a mirror of the society in which they are found. The marriage between the two can help us understand the implications of both. Understanding the history of education in Rwanda allows insight into the integrity of its people as well as the experiences children throughout many generations have endured.

Rwanda is a very small country, about the size of Maryland (roughly 10,000 square miles), located in the heart of Africa. Its history is rich in triumph, sadness, and hope. Since its territorial creation in the 15th century, oral traditions have always played a fundamental role in the Rwandan culture. There are no written records from this time period. In fact, little is known about the origins of the Rwandan state and its early educational system. Historians believe the original inhabitants were Kiga hill dwellers with a highly centralized state system, which began to expand based on agriculture and animal husbandry (Dorsey 1994). This group later would be identified as Hutu.

Concurrently, Tutsi herdsmen from the north and east also entered the area. It is believed that the initial contact between these two groups was peaceful. Some accounts believe that Tutsi herdsmen were pastoralists and the Hutu were farmers, and they coexisted peacefully at least until the end of the 15th century. The Tutsi eventually achieved domination over the socioeconomic and political systems, although they never constituted the majority. During this early era, the Tutsi represented approximately 14 percent of the total population, while the Hutu constituted about 85 percent. The remaining 1 percent of the original population consisted of the Twa, who were also known as pygmies (Dorsey 1994). The literature suggests that during this time, both Hutu and Tutsi children received a functional education, while previous generations had simply passed on skill sets for survival (Zeilberger 1961). The Hutu have always primarily been arable farmers, in contrast to the growing Tutsi population, who relied on their ability to raise livestock. This divide was later to lend itself to ethnic turmoil that was passed from one generation to the next through whatever functional educational framework existed.

When the Germans arrived in the Kingdom of Rwanda in the late 1890s, they found a unified, diplomatic nation. Europeans had largely imagined that they would find chaos and scattered tribes and were surprised by the intricate social order, with aristocrats and vassals. It was believed that order in the central African civilizations could only be due to European cousins: the Tutsi (Lemarchand 1970). This favoritism toward the Tutsi resulted in a shift of wealth, status, power, and education.

Although the Tutsi royal court lost its independence under the colonial occupation, Tutsi chiefs were able to gain power over the population, which at this time was mostly Hutu. After the First World War, the western provinces of German East Africa, Rwanda (Ruanda), and neighboring Burundi (Urundi) were given to Belgium to administer. In 1926, Belgian administrators removed a number of Hutu chiefs in northern Rwanda and replaced them with Tutsi. As a result of the power the Tutsi gained from the Belgians, they also received a superior education from the Belgian and German populace.

In 1933, the Belgian colonial authorities organized a census, from which teams of Belgian bureaucrats classified the whole population as Hutu, Tutsi, or Twa. Every Rwandan was counted and measured by height, the length of their nose, and the shape of their eyes. The Tutsi were taller, the Hutu were shorter and broader, and the Twa were pygmies and not of any importance to the Belgians. Some people were labeled Tutsi because they had more money or possessed the required number of cows, according to Belgian authorities. It was during this time that the two ethnic groups gained perception of their own separate identities.

Before 1946, the Tutsi monarchy opposed missionary schools because of the imposed conversion to Christianity. However, after years of obligatory Belgian ideologies, King Mutara consented to dedicate Rwanda to Christ the King. As a result, Catholic missions sprang up everywhere in Rwanda. With the missionaries came education, and with education came greater divides in Rwandan society. Most of the Hutu students who did acquire education found there were few jobs for them, and those who did eventually graduate from mission schools and seminaries took posts in the lower administration or became tradesmen and shopkeepers. Hutu women were not allowed an education at all.

By 1957, the Rwandan educational system was failing, with fewer than 3 percent of children finishing 6 years of primary school (Duarte 1995). In November 1959, violence erupted in Rwanda as a result of the Tutsi's acquired thirst for independence from Belgium. As a result, the Belgians decided to shift their support to favor the Hutu. The Belgians even went so far as to replace Tutsi chiefs with Hutu leaders and encouraged the Hutu's animosity toward the Tutsi. With the aid and support of Belgian military leaders, Hutu mobs killed the Tutsi people and burned Tutsi houses. Tens of thousands of Tutsi fled into exile in Uganda, Congo, Burundi, and Tanzania.

Temporary camps were set up, and the refugees were dependent on the government for assistance. In some Tutsi refugee camps, people were dying at a rate of 50 per day. In schools, children were forced to identify themselves as either Hutu or Tutsi at all times. Tutsi schoolchildren were often beaten or forced to leave school.

In April 1972, the Tutsi retaliated, and an estimated 200,000 Hutu were killed in a systematic slaughter. Many referred to this movement as "selective genocide," claiming that anyone who demonstrated potential Hutu leadership had been targeted. Every Hutu member of the cabinet and half the country's schoolteachers were killed.

It was during this time that an anti-Tutsi campaign was started by Hutu Major General Juvenal Habyarimana. In a coup d'état in July 1973, Habyarimana ousted President Gregoire Kayibanda and declared himself president of Rwanda. According to estimates from UNESCO, in 1985, the average rate of adult illiteracy was an astounding 53.4 percent, with males at 38.8 percent and females at 67.3 percent (Twagilimana 2007).

Over the years, the number of Rwandan refugees in neighboring states (Burundi, Uganda, and Tanzania) ballooned to well over a half million people. On October 1, 1990, angry at its continued exile and frustrated with Habyarimana's refusal to allow the Tutsi to return home to Rwanda, the Rwandan Patriotic Front attacked Rwanda from Uganda, thus igniting a civil war.

In April 1994, one of the most violent and efficient genocides in recent history occurred in Rwanda. In just 100 days, almost 1 million people were brutally killed. Most of the victims were Hutu moderates and Tutsi killed by Hutu extremists. Neighbors murdered neighbors, brothers killed brothers, people who were considered friends killed each other, usually with machetes or grenades.

The 1994 genocide dramatically impacted primary school education. UNICEF estimates that approximately 600 primary schools (32 percent of the pregenocide total) were destroyed, and 3,000 or more primary school teachers were lost (Newbury and Baldwin 2000). An estimated 300,000 children were slaughtered (Straus and Waldorf 2011).

Many Rwandan children still suffer the consequences of the genocide, with 101,000 children living in 42,000 households without an adult, due to the death or imprisonment of their parents (Straus and Waldorf 2011). These survivors also view education "as the only way out." They associate education with being able to get a job and provide for themselves as well as their families. Barriers to education largely stem from economic factors: the inability to pay for secondary school fees, materials, and transportation, and the need to earn a living to support their family. Some children lack money to purchase shoes that are required to attend school. Genocide survivors, whose fees are paid by Le Fonds d'Assistance aux Rescapés du Génocide (Fund for Assistance to Genocide Survivors), a fund set up by the Rwandan government, also report that the money does not always reach the schools at the beginning of the term, resulting in the students being turned away.

Under the current president, Paul Kagame, children are viewed as the hope for the future. In line with policy transitions elsewhere, the Rwandan government symbolically links children and children's rights to a national rebirth and re-imagined future. Large primary class sizes, teacher training, and an English language requisite for secondary graduation are at the forefront of challenges that most Rwandan schools now face. While no one will ever really understand the complexity of the genocide, there is no question that, in the minds of Rwandans, their future lies in their schools.

Technology in Rwandan Schools

It is in the context of this bloody history that the government and people of Rwanda have, in the past 15 years, begun to rebuild their nation. Beginning in 2000, the government established the VISION 2020 plan, with specific measurable short-, medium-, and long-term objectives (One Laptop Per Child 2011). This plan recognized the importance of a stable system of education in developing the nation's economy and addressing a dramatic level of poverty with the creation of the Economic Development and Poverty Reduction Strategy (EDPRS). More specifically, plans for an information and communications technology (ICT) policy for Rwanda resulted in the National Information and Communications Infrastructure (NICI) Policy and Plan that same year (Farrell and Isaacs 2007).

Six years of free compulsory primary education has been enforced since 2000, and some 94 percent of children are enrolled in primary schools. Since these initiatives, officials from other nations have praised ICT progress in Rwanda. According to One Laptop Per Child, the nonprofit American organization based in Miami, FL, whose mission is to equip children in developing countries with XO laptop computers, in just 5 years, more than 1,000 schools had at least one computer, some 40 schools in the capital city of Kigali had internet and connectivity, and more than 1,000 teachers had received computer training (One Laptop Per Child 2011).

By late 2007, approximately 750 XO computers had been distributed to primary-grade children in a rural school 2 hours outside of Kigali. Although the purpose of this initial rural distribution was to establish an infrastructure and observe children using the laptops, other changes were documented, including fewer students missing classes, higher student engagement in their schoolwork, and increased family involvement in children's education.

A year later, the government distributed some 10,000 laptops over all five of the country's provinces, and, in early 2010, the government purchased 65,000 laptops for primary-grade students in more than 150 schools across the country. Plans continued, with over 100,000 units anticipated for distribution in 2012, together with teacher-training sessions, student workshops, and community awareness meetings (One Laptop Per Child 2011).

It should be noted that, according to the Rwanda Education Statistics paper released by the Ministry of Education, the percentage of primary students who passed the national exam increased from 26.1 percent in 2005 to 82.6 percent in 2010, the percentage of "ordinary" secondary students who passed the national exam increased from 36.9 percent in 2005 to 84.9 percent in 2010, and the percentage of "advanced" secondary students who passed the national exam increased from 64.7 percent in 2005 to 87.4 percent in 2010 (Republic of Rwanda 2012).

Although there has been no specific relationship established between the distribution and use of laptops since 2005 and the increase in percentage of students passing the national exam during a similar period, the two trends have occurred simultaneously and warrant further study.

There are, of course, challenges to such a dramatic infusion of technology, especially in a developing nation. Many schools do not have reliable electricity or are outside the existing grid. Solar panels are being installed in some of these schools. Many educators understandably resist this new technology and the accompanying pedagogy shift. Consequently, professional development in this area requires encouragement, support, and assistance during and after training sessions. Teacher training sessions typically include administrators, and those who complete the training return to their schools and lead training sessions with teachers, students, and community members there. Constructive integration of the laptops into classroom instruction and learning is an ongoing goal for these training sessions, along with an understanding of how to maintain the laptops and what restrictions are necessary to maximize their use in a responsible manner.

The Ministry of Education in Rwanda is actively promoting the integration of technology into schools through the media, highlighting specific accomplishments over time. Older students at one school are teaching young students how to use the laptops for project work, beyond the traditional teacher-directed instructional model. Computer camps have been offered at some schools, and programs are in place at other schools that provide opportunities for students to use the laptops for projects away from school altogether (One Laptop Per Child 2011).

Partnerships that include nongovernmental organizations (NGOs), universities, foundations, and government agencies are a source of additional initiatives for sustaining the increased access to technology in schools across Rwanda. Volunteer service organizations are critical in providing personnel who can be taught to train educators at a school and a district level. Ultimately, the evaluation of these training sessions and their impact on student learning in schools must be systematically linked to the continued use of laptops and other forms of technology moving forward.

Technology for Learning in One Rural School

In 2010, the Rwandan Education Assistance Project (REAP), originally founded in 2008, entered into a partnership with the Duha Complex School in the Rwamagana district, the Green Hills Academy in Kigali, the Ministry of Education, local education officials, the Hameau des Jeunes orphanage, and several American schools and universities to collaboratively build a replicable model for rural education in Rwanda. Over 3,000 students, largely from poor families, live in the surrounding rural area and attend the Duha Complex School from kindergarten through high school. Only a few of the primary teachers have any education beyond high school, yet they each teach approximately 110 students every day (Figure 10.1). Although the official language of Rwanda is English, most teachers at Duha Complex School have limited English language skills and prefer to use Kinyarwandan, the native language of most Rwandans.

The principles and goals that guide the work of REAP and the Duha Complex School are as follows (Rwandan Education Assistance Project 2013):

- "Umwananimutware" – The child is chief: recognizing and valuing the potential of each child

- Actively engaging each child in the learning process by honoring the multiple ways children know and experience the world

- Using the local environment and community as sources of learning and curriculum development

- Building a physical environment that supports the safety, creativity, and physical well-being of all students, with a special emphasis on the privacy, health, and sanitation conditions for female students

- Creating a school climate that promotes respect, caring, responsibility, and trust to support the reconciliation process and democratic participation

- Strengthening the relationship between school and community

- Cultivating local leadership to sustain and enliven educational exchange

- Bridging resources between private independent schools and rural public schools

- Forging partnerships with multiple organizations to ensure collaboration and sustainability around food and healthcare

- Integrating the latest brain-based learning principles and their application to English language learning as well as to instructional strategies

- Promoting literacy by using local stories and folk tales as the source for published literature

- Introducing technology to support the delivery of curriculum

- Linking older children as mentors to younger children to promote learning and develop leadership

The first team of REAP workers arrived at the Duha Complex School during the summer of 2010. They included specialists in second

Figure 10.1   Children at the Duha Complex School
with a primary teacher

language learning, literacy, school leadership, pedagogy, counseling, and early learning. One priority established by this inaugural group was to build personal relationships with teachers, parents, administrators, and students at the school in order to establish some level of trust with the people we would be working with over the next several years. A second priority was to go as "blank slates," knowing nothing and learning as much as possible about the people and their neighborhoods, families, values, language, dreams, fears, and educational objectives.

Over a period of 3 weeks, relationships were formed, teachers from REAP and the Duha Complex School collaborated on classroom instruction, English language workshops were held, and collaborative work began on a strategic plan for the school. Smaller teams returned to the village in the spring of 2011 and winter of 2012, and larger teams worked there in the summers of 2011 and 2012. Priorities were determined by needs assessments conducted with school officials before every visit.

Electricity was limited to one or two rooms that were intermittently powered by a generator until November 2010, when REAP teamed with members of the community around the school to run power lines to the school. The power capacity improved but remained limited and unreliable. However, it prompted school officials and lead teachers to seek more access to technology for teachers and students. Two REAP partners, Rollins College in Winter Park, FL, and the Hackley School in Tarrytown, NY, contributed refurbished laptops that were brought to the school beginning in the summer of 2011.

Several projects were initiated beginning in the summer of 2011. A computer lab was established at the school, and school administrators selected a teacher to oversee activities in the lab. This lead teacher was provided with training to maintain the laptops and make minor repairs to the machines. A second initiative involved secondary teachers and students in an iMovie project (Figure 10.2). Secondary students and teachers were provided with Flip Cams and laptops, and created a series of videos highlighting accomplishments at the school and in the community. The secondary students then gathered upper-primary students in the lab and taught them how to transfer footage on the Flip Cams to the laptops, and eventually to larger screens for public presentations.

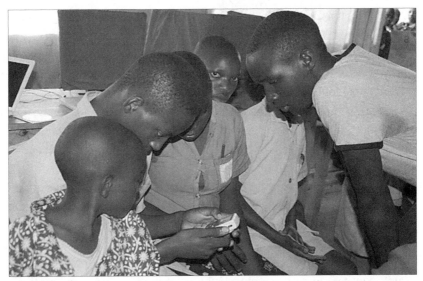

Figure 10.2   Secondary students teaching primary students to create iMovies using Flip Cams and laptops

Another initiative involved training teachers to care for the laptops and use essential software programs, including Word, Excel, and PowerPoint. The teacher who supervised the computer lab submitted a grant proposal to REAP, and a fundraiser organized by one of the authors provided support for the training of more than 40 primary and secondary teachers.

By the end of the summer of 2012, teachers were submitting evidence of classroom applications for the software programs. They were creating formal and informal assessments for students with Word, using Excel spreadsheets to maintain student records for their classes, and organizing attractive and creative PowerPoint presentations for subject area lessons, especially in the secondary classrooms. Following the training, the teacher in charge of the training provided REAP and Duha Complex School administrators with a report that included assessments of individual teachers, final costs, a reflective summary of the training experience, and priorities moving forward. Currently, there are approximately 30 laptops and desktop computers at the school being used by both teachers and students for a wide range of traditional academic tasks and innovative projects that extend student learning beyond the classroom. One example of this has been a group of students from both the primary and secondary schools who have collaborated on video productions, some of which are available on the REAP website (rwandaedu.org). They include music videos and productions that highlight the accomplishments of the Duha Complex School.

One Laptop Per Child has donated 600 XO laptops to the Duha Complex School, but a lack of training and a change in school leadership has slowed the integration of the laptops into the educational operations of the school. REAP has committed to a partnership with local officials that will increase the capacity of the electrical system to a point that the entire school can be more reliably powered on a daily basis. The new head teacher has been installed, and the educational goals for 2014 and beyond include continued computer training for teachers focused on applications in the classroom. Refurbished laptops will continue to be brought to Duha from donations secured by Rollins College, allowing teachers and students to use them throughout the school. Finally, additional projection systems will be brought to the school by members of REAP to facilitate the use of presentation technology in the classrooms.

Although the progress of technological integration at the Duha Complex School is slow, it is evident that teachers, administrators, students, and staff members are all working collaboratively on a variety of applications that are enhancing student learning and contributing to the overall success of the school in a challenging, impoverished, rural environment in Rwanda.

Into the Future

Rwanda has, with the help of One Laptop Per Child and other collaborative partners, introduced computer technology to students in schools nationwide at an impressive pace in recent years. Along with the introduction of computers to schools has come a new way of thinking about teaching and learning. Instead of sitting in crowded classrooms being lectured to for hours, students in some parts of Rwanda are creating their own learning, using laptops in and out of school to turn their own environments into learning opportunities with the help of technology.

This transformation of education does not come without its critics. Many are concerned that funds are being spent on computers that should be used to train teachers. Others point to the XO laptops, saying they consume too much electricity and are not compatible enough to be useful over time. Rwanda's electrical grid is struggling to keep pace with the emergence of technology, particularly in rural areas. Nonetheless, the excitement children have for the new technology and the learning they can accomplish with it is spreading, and government officials are watching.

With new leadership, more than 500 parents and members of the community participated in a school meeting at the Duha Complex School in February 2013. A new education liaison has been brought to the school by REAP, and together with another young coordinator who works with the school full time, they are collaborating with the new head teacher and other lead teachers there, pursuing goals that are focused on community, teaching and learning (specifically technology and English language learning), health and well-being, infrastructure, and partnerships. Teams of REAP volunteers will continue to work at the school, and student service groups are planned for the near future.

The integration of technology into the educational setting at the Duha Complex School has been possible because of a collaborative effort by local teachers and administrators, the district education officials, partner schools in Rwanda and the United States, and REAP. Once the XO laptops are in operation, there will be a greater integration with student learning in and out of school. Other rural schools in Rwanda can partner with the government, Rwandan schools closer to urban centers, parents and community leaders, and international organizations such as One Laptop Per Child and REAP to bring 21st-century technology to their teachers and students. The Rwanda Education NGO Coordination Platform (rencp.org), a coalition of organizations formed in 2009 and recently led by Plan International Rwanda and Wellspring Foundation of Education, is aimed at establishing and maintaining a collaboration of education partners, funding sources, and multidimensional agencies in support of education in Rwanda. These and other initiatives can help teachers and students throughout Rwanda gain access to unlimited information worldwide and open up opportunities for more Rwandan children to excel in learning at all levels.

Rwandan families and children in rural areas, not unlike rural populations in other nations, are often the last to benefit from innovative and progressive educational developments, including the integration of technology for learning. Bringing reliable electrical power to these rural areas is critical to the education of students in the 21st century. Connecting these young learners to the world beyond their villages is a key factor in strengthening the overall economic and social development of their regions and nations. Children in rural Rwanda are more connected to their world than ever before, and with continued partnerships like those outlined here, the future of technology-assisted education in Rwanda is bright!

References

Barnett, Michael N. 2002. *Eyewitness to a Genocide: The United Nation and Rwanda*. London: Cornell University Press.

Dorsey, Learthen. 1994. *Historical Dictionary of Rwanda*. London: The Scarecrow Press.

Duarte, Mary T. 1995. "Education in Ruanda-Urundi, 1946–61." *Historian: A Journal or History* 57(2): 275–284.

Ember, Melvin, and Carol R. Ember. (Eds.) 2001. *Countries and Their Cultures*. New York: Macmillan Reference.

Farrell, Glen, and Shafika Isaacs. 2007. *Survey of ICT and Education in Africa: A Summary Report, Based on 53 Country Surveys*. Washington, DC: infoDev/World Bank. www.infodev.org/en/Publication.353.htm.

Gall, Timothy L., and Susan B. Gall. 1999. *Rwanda: Worldmark Chronology of the Nations*. New York: Cengage Gale.

Lemarchand, René. 1970. *Rwanda and Burundi*. London: Pall Mall Press.

Lye, Keith. 2006. *Philip's World Factbook*, 4th ed. New York: Philips Paperback.

Melvern, Linda. 2000. *A People Betrayed: The Role of the West in Rwanda's Genocide*. London: Zed Books.

Newbury, Catharine and Hannah Baldwin. 2000. *Aftermath: Women in Post Genocide Rwanda*. Washington, DC: Center for Development Information and Evaluation, U.S. Agency for International Development. pdf.usaid.gov/pdf_docs/pnacj323.pdf.

Newbury, David. 2009. *The Land Beyond the Mists: Essays in Identity and Authority in Precolonial Congo and Rwanda*. Athens, OH: Ohio University Press.

One Laptop Per Child. 2011. *Transforming Society Through Access to a Modern Education. (Country Case Study: Rwanda)*. Miami: One Laptop Per Child Association. wiki.laptop.org/images/2/28/Rwanda_Report.pdf.

Pottier, Johan. 2002. *Re-Imagining Rwanda: Conflict, Survival, and Disinformation in the Late Twentieth Century*. Cambridge, UK: Cambridge University Press.

Republic of Rwanda. 2012. *Rwanda Education Statistics*. Kigali: Ministry of Education. www.mineduc.gov.rw/IMG/pdf/2011_RWANDA_EDUCATION_STATISTICS.pdf.

Rittner, Carol, John K. Roth, and Wendy Whitworth. (Eds.). 2004. *Genocide in Rwanda: Complicity of the Churches?* St. Paul, MN: Paragon House.

Rwandan Education Assistance Project. 2013. "Principles and Goals." rwandaedu.org/about/mission-vision.

Smith, David L. 2011. *Less Than Human: Why We Demean, Enslave, and Exterminate Others*. New York: St. Martin's Press.

Stearns, Jason K. 2011. *Dancing in the Glory of Monsters: The Collapse of the Congo and the Great Way of Africa*. New York: Public Affairs.

Straus, Scott and Lars Waldorf. 2011. *Remaking Rwanda: State Building and Human Rights After Mass Violence*. Madison, WI: The University of Wisconsin Press.

Tanner, R.E.S. 1971. "Priestly Classes in East and Central Africa." *Heythrop Journal* 12(2): 175–191.

Totten, Samuel and Rafiki Ubaldo. (Eds.). 2011. *We Cannot Forget: Interviews With Survivors of the 1994 Genocide in Rwanda*. New Brunswick, NJ: Rutgers University.

Twagilimana, Aimable. 2007. *Historical Dictionary of Rwanda*. Lanham, MD: Scarecrow Press.

Vanisina, Jan M. 1985. *Oral Traditions as History*. Madison, WI: The University of Wisconsin Press.

Zeilberger, Yehudah. 1961. "Functional Education." Translated by Doron Zeilberger. In *Educational Encyclopedia (Encyclopedia Khinukhit)*, Vol. 1, 706–710. Jerusalem: The Israel Ministry of Education and Mossad Bialik.

CHAPTER 11

Galapagos ICE

Denise Cummings

In December 2007, in coordination with the nonprofit organization, Galapagos ICE (GICE), 29 students from Rollins College in Winter Park, FL, participated in a field study service-learning and leadership course called "Activism 101" on Santa Cruz, Galapagos, Ecuador. Led by a Rollins faculty member, a student affairs coordinator, an instructional technology administrator, and several staff members, and chronicled by two professional videographers, the Rollins students were charged with teaching English language classes and computer skills to secondary school students at El Colegio Nacional Miguel Ángel Cazares on the archipelago's most populous island.

As part of its innovative liberal arts curriculum, field study programs at Rollins are defined as emphasizing experiential learning. Faculty and staff member teams at the college design their field study programs to take advantage of the location and work to integrate more traditional coursework with hands-on experiences that will enhance the curriculum and provoke discussion and active engagement with the subject of the course (Rollins College n.d.). All field study programs incorporate traditional assignments, exams, papers, lectures, and discussions.

Activism 101, a service-learning field study experience, was designed to build on Rollins' commitment to social responsibility by combining a volunteer and service-learning focused travel opportunity. The Rollins effort was led by Les Lloyd, Activism 101 instructor and field study leader and former chief information officer; Denise K. Cummings, assistant professor of Critical Media and Cultural Studies; Doug Little, former director of First Year Programs; and Troy Thomason, Carrie Schulz, and Joe Hughes of Information Technology. Matthew F. Reyes of Exploration Solutions and Paul Gramaglia of PG Film Entertainment provided videography.

An Organization With Vision

While researching service-learning opportunities in Ecuador for American students, Lloyd found Emily Pozo, an American-born activist who had met her husband, the late Mauricio Pozo, in Ecuador. Recognizing that poor economic conditions for Galapagos residents and lack of basic social services, such as education and healthcare, function as silent accomplices in the ecological deterioration of the islands (galapagosice.org), the couple selected the island of Santa Cruz, the most inhabited of the islands, and established GICE in 2007, the same year the Galapagos Archipelago was designated as the first United Nations Educational, Scientific and Cultural Organization (UNESCO) World Heritage Site.

ICE stands for "Immerse, Connect and Evolve," which "is what the organization wants to achieve for its volunteers on the one hand, and for the local population on the other hand: Immerse in the local culture and living habits for the volunteers, and immerse in GICE's projects for the locals; Connect with the local people, their way of living, and the life on the island, for the volunteers, and connect with the volunteers and the organization, for the locals; Evolve personally through the wonderful and impacting experience volunteers have during their stay in this unique place, and also make the island and its inhabitants, and Evolve thanks to the work that the volunteers are conducting (Li, Lozano, and Vaquette 2012).

GICE envisions a Galapagos community in which all individuals have access to adequate education and healthcare, and one that is viewed by all as a valued partner in efforts to protect the fragile ecology of the islands. The organization seeks to help accomplish sustainable development in Galapagos by empowering local residents to take control of their own futures, which, the organization believes "are inextricably entwined with the future of the fragile Galapagos" ecology (Galapagos ICE, "About Us" n.d.). GICE believes that by valuing the local population, and extending to them the opportunities afforded by education and access to medical care, local residents will be empowered to take more active roles in the guardianship of their fragile environment. For Lloyd and the organizing team, GICE emerged as the ideal organization to integrate Rollins' commitment to social responsibility with the mission of the newly founded island organization.

Uniting Communities

GICE identified needs at Miguel Ángel Cazares, a school situated in the densely developed town of Puerto Ayora. Within the bounded spaces of the school's traditional walled classrooms, open-air classrooms, and varied school playgrounds, the Rollins students focused their language lesson plans on conservation and sustainability of the rare ecosystem found in the Galapagos, thus reinforcing the islands' established codes of eco-tourism to the very people who will manage the islands in the future: the young students.

Eager to learn their islands' conservation rules in English, the Colegio students responded with overwhelming enthusiasm to the Rollins students; ultimately, the two student groups were immersed in an open exchange of both academic ideas and socio-cultural traditions such as song and dance. During recess periods, the student groups merged for impromptu games of basketball and soccer; several younger students avidly followed the videographers, who, in turn, gave them personal digital photography and videography lessons, joined them in playing video games, and together browsed websites, such as NASA.

In addition to teaching the eighth- through 13th-graders (grade 13 is for students who plan to go to college), the entire Rollins group donated more than one dozen personal computers, four laptops, three digital video cameras, a projector, and sundry items for the school's library such as textbooks and board games. With assistance from several Rollins students and a number of willing Colegio students, the Rollins IT staff installed all of the computers, complete with software programs such as Photoshop; equipped the school with wireless internet; rewired the school's English Language Lab; and left behind additional cabling and tools for sustainable network support. All of the students' and instructors' experiences were chronicled on digital video. The field study course, a component of the semester-long Activism 101, also achieved two important firsts: Rollins College was the first American college or university to visit El Colegio Nacional Miguel Ángel Cazares and the first to work with GICE with the specific goals of teaching the English language to secondary school students and to actively involve the Galapagos community in efforts to preserve the natural wonders of the islands.

Since 2007, GICE has evolved as an organization, achieving formal recognition as a nongovernmental organization (NGO) by the Ecuadoran government and nonprofit status as a U.S. 501(c)(3) international charity and expanding its undertaking of sustainable projects (Li, Lozano, and Vaquette 2012). Its growth as a health and human services organization is marked by its resilience and responsiveness to the changing needs of the community. Three overarching campaigns focus on the organization's three major areas of work: health, education, and green (a term denoting conservation and sustainability). Volunteer groups, comprised of medical and educational professionals as well as high school and college students from around the world, have undertaken a variety of projects, from medical brigades to the development of library collections to rehabilitation of playgrounds, which are primary centers of social life, relaxation, and fun for children on Santa Cruz because formal recreation programs and centers are very limited (galapagosice. org/?page_id=45). By 2013, 510 volunteers from 23 countries had given 33,484 volunteer hours to the health and education of the human residents on Santa Cruz.[1] The Rollins group was at the forefront.

The Impact of Rollins

Four years after the Rollins group worked at the Puerto Ayora school, Marcos Peralvo, principal of Miguel Ángel Cazares, was asked about the impact on the school by the Rollins visitors and their 2007 activities at the school. The following excerpt[2] characterizes Peralvo's perceptions of the initial and enduring impact of the 2007 visit:

> For the students of Miguel Ángel Cazares National High School, this was an enriching experience because it allowed them to share their lives through the activities and games. At the educator level, it allowed me to get to know the different technologies being used in places different than our own home. For instance, it is highly important to have this kind of information and culture exchange when the chance is given.

In response to the following specific questions, Peralvo provided feedback:

> *What have been the major benefits to the school from the connectivity to the internet Rollins provided?*

[Prior to the visit by the group from Rollins College], the institution only possessed eight computers that didn't work properly; for this reason, [the donation from Rollins College] was one of the most important computer equipment contributions that the institution has received.

Does the school keep using internet access?

Yes.

For what type of educational objectives do you use it?

- Virtual space management
- Information access
- Instructional support material
- Class lessons
- Information Communications Technology (ICT) management

These educational objectives Peralvo identified are significant in that it was not until 2011 that the International Telecommunication Union (ITU) reported that all the main piers on the islands received free internet for the first time in history. ITU further reported that 31 schools benefited—El Colegio Nacional Miguel Ángel Cazares among them—noting:

The main event was held in Santa Cruz, in public school Galo Plaza Lasso ... later the authorities made a visit to the national school Miguel Angel Cazares and national college Galapagos and finally at 16:30 the system was inaugurated WiFi wireless on the pier in Puerto Baquerizo Moreno San Cristobal. On Friday, they will visit the school fiscomisional Pedro Pablo Andrade, where it will be also delivered equipment and connectivity. (International Telecommunication Union 2011)

The institutions that participated actively in the implementation of the connectivity project were the Council of Provincial Government of Galapagos, the Ministry of Education, the National Telecommunications Corporation, and the Ministry of Telecommunication and Information Society (International Telecommunication Union 2011).

The Galapagos Islands are famous for the diversity of the wildlife and the extraordinary environmental balance required to support this unique corner of the world. Consequently, in the 21st century, a great number of environmental initiatives and volunteering opportunities spread across the archipelago, which the 2007 partnership between GICE and Rollins exemplifies. However, due to strict laws from the Children and Adolescence Code (Código de Niñez y Adolescencia actualizado, galapagosice.org/wp-content/uploads/2013/01/cc3b3digo-de-nic 3b1ez-y-adolescencia-actualizado1.pdf), volunteers in the schools cannot work directly with the students unless they are contracted by the educational institution (Galapagos ICE, "Education" n.d.).

Today, GICE education programs are mainly mainstreamed through the organization's Healthy Lifestyle initiatives. This alternative angle is designed to bring a sense of consciousness of health promotion to the people of the islands. Thus, the GICE–Rollins College–El Colegio Nacional Miguel Ángel Cazares partnership stands as a unique historic collaboration inspired by the vision of the local Dirección de Educación (local head of education) and social justice activists from two countries and continents.

Endnotes

1. Personal correspondence with Marcos Peralvo, 19 September 2011.

2. Email correspondence with Judith Smith, Board of Directors, GICE, 13 June 2013.

References

Galapagos ICE. n.d. "About Us." galapagosice.org/?page_id=9.

———. n.d. "Education." galapagosice.org/?page_id=71.

International Telecommunication Union. 2011. "SIs Newslog – Galapagos Residents and Tourists Have Free Wireless Internet – Ecuador." www.itu.int/ITU-D/sis/ newslog/2011/01/16/GalapagosResidentsAndTouristsHaveFreeWirelessInternet Ecuador.aspx.

Li, Poyi, Juan Jesus Silva Lozano, and Valentine Vaquette. 2012. "Fundraising, Marketing, and Operational Support for an NGO in the Galapagos Islands." Vlerick Leuven Gent Management School. Ghent, Belgium, 2012: 4.

Rollins College. n.d. "Field Study Program." www.rollins.edu/int-programs/programs/ field-study-programs/index.html.

CHAPTER 12

A Service-Learning Novice Finds His Way

Les Lloyd

For a very long time, I tried to figure out how to combine my passions for travel, teaching, and technology. I came up with the idea of bringing discarded college computers to a developing nation, setting up a computer lab in a middle or high school, and teaching computer skills (we later added English to the mix). I originally intended it for Buenos Aires (or some other South American location I had never visited), but it turned out summer vacation for schools there clashed with our ideal time to visit, which was the 10 days immediately following finals after the fall term. We settled on Mexico, but I wanted someplace other classes were not already visiting and a little off the beaten path. Coincidentally, a lunchtime conversation resulted in a recommendation that San Miguel de Allende might be a good location.

Location, Location, Location

I had some basic requirements for a location. First, it had to be no more than 8 hours door-to-door. I didn't want to waste a day on either end of the trip traveling or recovering from the travel; it was important that we arrive ready to work. Second, the timing had to be right, as already mentioned. Third, I wanted to teach in a rural area, but I wanted us to be in a town where students could experience the culture and history of the local area. Finally, the area had to be safe. San Miguel fit all these criteria: It is a beautiful colonial town with a significant arts sector and with rural schools fairly close by (a decade ago, these schools were 45 minutes away; new roads recently facilitated that travel in about 20 minutes). Other nearby towns, such as Dolores Hidalgo, provided a less polished location for students to explore and learn. San Miguel is located between Mexico City and the U.S. border, hours away from both and the troubles that exist there.

Ready to Go, Right?

With approvals from the appropriate committee and deans, I figured we were set. Little did I know that it is not very easy to get in touch with school administrators in Mexico, as they are wary of being solicited by salespeople, and most schools only have one phone, if they have one at all. We called and wrote to every middle school in San Miguel and didn't get a single response. After trying for days, we got one person on the phone who sounded interested; we made an appointment to call back, but he never called or was available for us to speak to again.

With urgings from some on campus to locate in Merida because we had connections there, I was more determined than ever to make a connection in San Miguel (I tend to not want to follow conventions). I opened the town's website and copied every email address on the site (for realtors, artists, merchants, etc.). I pleaded for anyone who knew a teacher to have them contact me. Several people sent messages of encouragement, but only one had a concrete suggestion. A former professional figure skater (who reminded me while in San Miguel that she still skates into her 60s), who now teaches dance and movement to schoolchildren, put me in touch with a teacher at Naciones Unidas, a private school. We were finally able to move forward.

After a long weekend visit in July, I was convinced that San Miguel was the right place. I scouted out the town and located a person who specialized in logistics for groups coming from the U.S. San Miguel de Allende is located near the geographical center of Mexico, about 4 hours north of Mexico City—far enough away from there and from the problems at the U.S./Mexico border that I could convince the risk management folks that it was safe for us to go. Students were recruited from the incoming class based on those who had several years of high-school Spanish and indicated an interest or proficiency in computers and studying off-campus.

Preparation

My class of freshman students arrived on campus in mid-August. As the first off-campus study program for first-semester students, we were breaking new ground. Many parents attended the orientation session for my class; several others called or contacted me by email with questions. We were on our way.

During the fall term, the students read three books: *FrontPage for Dummies* (For Dummies, 2000), *The Mexicans: A Personal Portrait of People* (Harper, 2002), and *On Mexican Time: A New Life in San Miguel* (Broadway Books, 2001). The first book, *FrontPage for Dummies*, was used to teach the class how to build websites. Once a week, during the first half of the term, we had an IT staff member come to class to teach these skills.

The Mexicans profiled about 18 individual Mexicans in the late 1980s. It was a great introduction to the issues that faced Mexico at that time and, indeed, still today: pollution, poverty, corruption, and education. The issues were presented as they impacted the individuals; for example, a maid was profiled who had to take several buses to work each day, a trip that took 2 hours in each direction. Paid average wages, she would barely make enough to pay for the transportation and other expenses to get to work, but the author of the book paid her above-average wages. Similarly, students learned about the political system, the issues limiting environmental protection, and more. In final papers, students updated each of these profiles to the present.

On Mexican Time was written by a California couple who came to San Miguel on vacation and never left. It described the feel of the town and how it welcomed them, their search for a home, and the decision to fix up a 300-year-old home.

Spanish professor (and co-editor of this book) Gabriel Barreneche came to class weekly during the second half of the term to teach technical Spanish to the students. Using a *Jeopardy*-like game, he introduced students to the Spanish translations of *mouse*, *internet*, *click*, and much more. Using additional exercises and websites he provided, the students were able to study these terms so they were ready to use them in Mexico. Professor Barreneche helped them hone their presentation skills, too, by watching their practice teaching sessions and offering suggestions. Students also received handouts on current events in Mexico and background information on central Mexico and San Miguel.

Education professor Scott Hewit came to several classes to work with students on their pedagogy. He coached them on how to teach sixth- to ninth-grade students, how to engage them, create lesson plans, and more.

Most importantly, both faculty members helped the students develop a sense of what it's like to be in front of a group of children and responsible for their learning. One thing the three of us noticed during this practice time was that the students needed coaching on group dynamics. Using the resources of our Personal Counseling Center and Healthy Campus initiative, we started to build the trust and teamwork needed for successful group teaching.

We also added a laptop specialist from IT to the group. He registered for the travel class and was assigned a group to work with in class. His role would be both to work with the group that would be teaching the students computer repair and also to provide computer support for the laptops we were bringing to Mexico.

During the term, the students were also responsible for raising funds to pay the school for the used laptops (we stopped doing this after the first year, since we ensured that the laptops could not be used anywhere on campus). Students raised funds by having a car wash and selling Mexican craft items and photography by yours truly. They sold items at new student check-in, during family weekend, and in the library all semester. They also had booths at the local Winter Park Farmer's Market and the Winter Park Crafts Show. Each student wrote letters to family and friends asking for donations.

By the end of the term, the students, divided into three groups, created websites on basic computer skills, an introduction to FrontPage, and advanced FrontPage skills. These websites would be their outlines to teach from and reference materials they could leave behind for the students and teachers. All information on the sites was provided in both English and Spanish.

Working together in my course for a semester gave the students a great chance to bond and problem-solve together while learning their way around during their first term in college. But they were new enough to college so as not to forget the challenges that confronted them and their teachers back in high school.

Students as Teachers: Teaching Students to Lead Classes and Cope With Unforeseen Situations

Our contact Carlos made arrangements for us to teach in two schools. One, the school where he teaches second grade, is private. The other, located about 15 miles outside of San Miguel in "rancher country," is public.

Naciones Unidas (United Nations) is where Carlos teaches. Located in a rented home, the school educates children in first through eighth grades. Classes range from eight to 20 students. Tuition at the school is $140 (U.S.) a month, with about 20 percent of students receiving scholarships. The students are split between those of U.S. and those of Mexican heritage. Students are bilingual, and classes are taught in both languages; however, most of the teachers speak Spanish as their first language, so most classes are taught in Spanish. There seems to be no boundaries, prejudices, or rifts between the students. They play and work together well. The students are close to their teachers and the principal. While the school had two computers when we arrived, it is not equipped like schools in the U.S. There is no heat; students wear sweaters and coats all day. Assemblies and recreation take place in a dusty yard with trees blocking efforts to play real games of soccer. The house's kitchen doubles as its science lab. The school is located in a residential neighborhood of similar and larger homes, most of which are unoccupied during the week but visited on the weekends by their owners from Mexico City. Professor Hewit remarked that the principal is well-versed in Western teaching theory and runs a first-rate program.

The second school, *Telesecundaria* 1005, is in the community of Soasnávar. Reachable only by a dirt and rock road off the main road to Jalpa, the community and school are quite poor. There are two classrooms and no offices, and outhouses are located about 100 yards from the classroom building. A satellite dish provides the school's only connectivity to the outside; there are no phone lines, cable, or internet connections. There are three electrical outlets in the school. The school yard is large, with a concrete pad for game playing or school gatherings. There is no lunchroom, no ball field, and no science lab. Located about 15 miles from downtown San Miguel, it is in stark contrast to the beauty and history of this town.

To prepare for our visit, the community built what we would consider a makeshift shed on the side of the school building (on the left of Figure 12.1). One-third of the students were moved from the classrooms in the main building into this "new" classroom so we could comfortably teach about 25 students at a time in each classroom. Maps and other teaching

Figure 12.1   *Telesecundaria* 1005

materials were taped to the walls, and student desks and chairs sat right on the dusty ground.

The college students were split into three groups. One would teach at the private school and two at the public. Every couple of days they switched, so that all the students could experience both schools. The three teachers also rotated between the schools, and we ensured that our IT person and I were each at different locations on any given day to deal with any technical problems or questions.

Students approached their teaching tasks with confidence. On the first day at the public school in Soasnávar, we approached two different schools with all our materials and supplies before we found the correct one tucked into the hillside off the "main" road, accessible only by a rocky dirt path. The college students split up into inside and outside groups so that some of the schoolchildren could be outside getting famil- iar with their new teachers while others set up the computers indoors. They were setting up to teach almost 120 students in three groups.

The college students quickly built a rapport with the students, and many formed ties with individual students that lasted through the week.

Indoors, our students were charged with connecting seven or eight laptops to one electrical outlet (there should have been more computers, but several were stuck in unavailable luggage). They created a center island of computers with surge protectors and extension cords to link them together. After dealing with the power and readying the computers, they called the students in for their first computer lesson.

In the first classroom, one of our students led her group with introductions. Using a map she brought from home and cutouts of objects representative of locations in the U.S., students in her group introduced themselves and indicated on the map where they were from. They then involved the local students in identifying key areas in the U.S. We asked the pupils about their families. Surprisingly, more than half of their parents worked in the U.S. while the students lived with other family members.

In the second classroom, after brief introductions, students went right to the computers (Figure 12.2). Most of the students in Soasnávar had never seen a computer before. To get them interested, the college students showed them solitaire and pinball and let them loose on the computers to get used to keyboarding, using the mouse, and the general features of Windows. Very few local students understood English, so all teaching and assistance was done in Spanish or with charades, depending on the comfort level of the instructors.

In both classes, it became obvious to the college students that teaching webpage design would have little meaning to these students. Without a telephone line or even satellite phone access, we could not demonstrate the web to them, so creating webpages seemed pointless. After getting to know the local students, the college students decided to concentrate on basic computer skills and the use of Microsoft Word. Later in the week, we learned that the school regularly sent a newsletter home, prepared by the principal. It discussed school activities; the students brought the newsletter home and read it to their families, many of whom could not read. It was decided that we would change the objective of the week to teach the students to create their own newsletters using Word in two-column mode and adding clip art and photographs that the students could take using the two digital cameras we were leaving with them. With this new objective, our students spent the rest of the week working on that task. By Friday, almost every student had substantially completed a newsletter. With the printer we

Figure 12.2   A rare moment at *Telesecundaria* 1005 with one student
per computer; on most days in Soasnávar, two to four
students huddled around each computer

were leaving for the school, our students worked to print all the newsletters for students to take home on this last day of classes before the
holiday break.

One of our students, Marina ('07), wrote in her journal:

> Once we set up the computers and the kids went in the room,
> I felt like I was Santa Claus. It was like giving them the best
> presents of their lives, but at the same time giving them a
> better future. They were so happy to be given this oppor-
> tunity that I started to cry. I know some people say I'm an
> emotional person, but how can you not be sensitive to these
> kids who have nothing and [are getting] a shot at learning
> something that only the privileged get to experience? That's
> exactly what this trip was supposed to be all about for me; to
> give these children an opportunity to learn what we all think
> is so basic. And I think we did just that.

At the private school *Naciones Unidas,* our students had a very different experience, though with equally satisfying results. At this school, our students were encouraged to speak English to help the school's students with their English skills. Sometimes the college students spoke Spanish and the school students spoke English so that everyone got to practice their second language. The school had just installed a cable modem, so access to the internet was available on one computer in the room they had designated their computer lab, probably designed originally as a bedroom in the home. Set up with three 6-foot tables, the room could accommodate about 10 students comfortably. With the five laptop computers our students were donating and a switch connected to the cable modem, each computer in the room had internet access. Like most buildings in San Miguel, the building had no heat, so sweaters, coats, and hats were the norm for most of the day during cold spells.

We were to teach sixth- and seventh-graders at this school and set out to do so on Monday. Our students quickly bonded with their pupils, since class sizes in these grades were each under 10 students. The sixth-graders were eager to learn, and the Rollins students quickly introduced themselves and started their task. Most of the students had good computer skills, so few basics were needed. The sixth-grade class went almost entirely according to plan; we spent the week teaching Front-Page and having the students each create a personal webpage with links, photos, and information about themselves or their interests.

In the seventh grade, there were three students who already had websites, so the instructors again changed course somewhat and taught FrontPage to those students who were not familiar with it and Power-Point to those students who were. They discussed the use of PowerPoint for presentations, and the students used that tool to create a presentation about themselves or their interests.

Daily morning and afternoon briefings and logistics discussions kept the group informed of schedule updates and other plans. Each evening, student groups met to pass on information about what they had accomplished to the next group teaching the students they had just taught. Lesson plans were due each night; napkins were an acceptable form of submission for their teaching plans. Professor Hewit reviewed plans and helped students make adjustments as needed.

Each day at Soasnávar, parents from the community came to work on a new storage/computer building (Figure 12.3). Residents donated

Figure 12.3   New storage/computer building at *Telesecundaria* 1005

materials and labor to create the facility in which the students would be able to use the computers we provided.

The End of Our Teaching Week

After 5 days of preparing, teaching, discussing, and writing, team members were exhausted but exhilarated. They had successfully completed their tasks and had the gratitude of not only their pupils but the principals and the town as well. Everywhere we went, people had heard of the project and encouraged us.

For our last day with the local students, we prepared scrapbooks. We also prepared certificates for each of the 150 or so students we taught. The students at *Naciones Unidas* invited our students to their Christmas Pageant, which we had watched them prepare for all week. We expected to make a presentation at the show, handing out the certificates and presenting the scrapbook we prepared to students and parents. Unfortunately, we had the wrong theater, so when we arrived at the show, we had missed our cue. We did, however, get to present the certificates at the end of the show and give the school a copy of the presentation to view on their own.

One student, Kate ('05), wrote in her journal:

> I knew this pageant was important to them, because they had been working so hard on it all week. It was also important to me, though, as it would be the last time I would ever see these kids. I was emotional that day because I would truly miss them, and I also found out that day that they would truly miss me.

After spending a week together, many Rollins students bonded with their pupils. At the Christmas show, we watched as faculty and students performed for the audience and said good-bye after the certificate presentations.

At Soasnávar, the school had special plans for us. Once we finished working with students on their newsletters and training faculty on the use and care of the laptops, we joined the entire school in the yard, where desks and chairs had been moved for an assembly. It was very touching as they performed for us in English and Spanish and invited us to participate in the assembly (Figure 12.4).

Student Sylvia ('07) wrote in her journal:

> We passed out the certificates to each student, and Les said a few words about us and the accomplishment of our mission. We handed out the scrapbooks, Gabriel gave them a taping of the Posada, and Joe gave them T-shirts. Just when we thought that was it, Francisco (the principal) turned the tables and gave each one of us a certificate for a job well done. They also had piñatas for us. At this moment, we made it clear to the entire school that we were donating the computers to them. The screams of joy from both sides were tremendous. The kids came around and wished each and every one of us a Merry Christmas and handed out Christmas cards. By now, Marina and I were crying like babies! It was so overwhelming to realize how much they appreciated us. It seemed like such a little thing that we were doing but it had such a HUGE effect! As we said farewell to everyone, the most important conversation was the one Marina and I had with Francisco. He wanted it to be clear that we made a huge impact on the entire school because

Figure 12.4   Rollins students hand out certificates to the
Telesecundaria 1005 students in Soasnávar

we were promoting a positive future for the entire school. He
said that the slogan on the iron-on shirts we presented was
absolutely true: We were making a huge difference to them.
(We created T-shirts for the teachers at the schools. They had
pictures of our class on them and the phrase "Making a difference," in Spanish). He was eternally grateful for all of our
hard work, and the fact that we gave them the computers was
minimal compared to the connections that were made with
the children. He said that if he kept on watching us cry, he
himself was going to tear up. Marina and I walked out of the
public school with tears of joy and sadness because of all we
put into the project and what we took from it. We were the
last to hop onto the bus, and the beginning of the ride back
to the hotel was pretty silent; it was a time to reflect on what
just had happened.

Wrap-Up

As the first of what has become an almost annual event, this experience was very special to the three leaders. The amount of planning that goes into a trip like this, ensuring that logistics are in place (e.g., students have passports and shots, flights back home, food, lodging, and a budget that works), can be challenging. But discussing and reading the students' thoughts on how the week went really made everything worthwhile; those comments are consistent from year to year. Students talk about changing their life goals, wanting to teach, join the Peace Corps, or do more international work. We were not naïve enough to think that our week of English and computer skills was going to change every middle-school student we worked with. But we did think that if just a couple of students who would not ordinarily go to high school decided to go, and if just one went to college, then that made everything worth it. And each time we travel, those are our goals: that a significant number of our students are touched by the experience, that some reconsider their career options, and that there exists the possibility of positively impacting the lives of the Mexican students.

Since the first trip, I have returned to San Miguel with students several times. Ecuador was added as another location, and we replicated this project in Cuenca, Otavalo, and the Galapagos Islands.

In 2012, I brought a student group back to the same school in Soasnávar that we had worked with 10 years prior. Astoundingly, they still had all 10 computers we donated! The school had expanded significantly, and the teachers and principal were all different, but they had heard of our previous visit and embraced us enthusiastically. They had enough space this time so they didn't have to build a temporary classroom for us, and the students did have more English and computer skills than their counterparts had a decade earlier. But there was still plenty for us to do, and we reaffirmed that the project could be repeated almost anywhere with similar results.

Final Thoughts

Les Lloyd

The projects described in this book have a couple of common themes. Their authors/organizers took a chance on something they believed in and went outside their comfort zones to create a learning experience for their students and a benefit to those they visited. Technology is a common theme, whether teaching technology on laptops or iPads or using communication technology to bring together students across distances to collaborate on or view a project as it unfolds. While the logistics of trip planning, recruiting students, and getting the necessary approvals, budgets, and so on can be daunting, in reality, these are projects that could originate from virtually any college campus. When we designed the computer/English class scenario, it was specifically designed (and we received grant support) to be replicable. That is, every college has leftover computers; every developing nation has training needs; and service-learning can be tremendously beneficial to our college students.

The tools are there and the resources can be found. (I have baked a lot of cheesecakes to raise money for my students' trips.) It just takes some people who want to make a difference and potentially change lives. I hope you are one of those people.

About the Contributors

Mariana Amatullo is vice president in the Designmatters department at Art Center College of Design. Amatullo founded Designmatters, based in Pasadena, CA, in 2001. As the lead of the program and at the helm of the Designmatters concentration in art and design for social impact, she develops strategic educational partnerships and oversees a portfolio of research collaborations, communication campaigns, exhibitions, and publications that enhance Art Center's commitment to be at the forefront of international design education and contribute solutions to humanitarian issues of critical urgency. In 2012, *Fast Company* magazine listed Amatullo as one of its "Design 50."

Denise Cummings is associate professor and chair of Critical Media and Cultural Studies at Rollins College. Her teaching and research focus on film history, theory, and criticism; American and American Indian film and literature; and media and cultural studies. She is editor of *Visualities: Perspectives on Contemporary American Indian Film and Art* (Michigan State University Press 2011) and co-editor of *Seeing Red, Hollywood's Pixeled Skins: American Indians and Film* (Michigan State University Press 2013). Cummings regularly teaches community-based service-learning courses. She has curated numerous film programs and serves on selection committees and juries for several film festivals, including the Florida Film Festival.

Dr. Patricia Davis-Wiley holds an AB and MA in French from the University of California and a MEd and EdD in curriculum and instruction from the University of Houston. She taught high school French and Spanish, French at Baylor University, and World Language Methods classes at the University of Houston. She is presently professor of world languages and English as a second language education at the University of Tennessee (Department of Theory and Practice in Teacher Education), where she coordinates the World Language Education program and directs PhD students in ESL education. Dr. Davis-Wiley was a visiting faculty member at Chuncheon National University of Education, Chuncheon, South Korea, teaching in the Intensive English Institutes (1996–2002) and an invited professor in January 2011. Her research interests and publications include content-enriched FLES (Foreign Language in the Elementary Schools), the impact of world language instruction on academic success, and innovations in instructional technology in the L2 classroom.

Dan Gottlieb and **Penny Herscovitch** are Los Angeles-based designers and design educators. Together they lead the design studio Padlab and co-teach in the Environmental Design department at Art Center College of Design in Pasadena, CA. Padlab's work encompasses materials research and innovation, illumination, and spatial installation design. The pair has lectured and taught internationally, and their work has been published extensively. Herscovitch also conducts research and writes for renowned institutions and firms, including Morphosis Architects. In 2003, Gottlieb received his Master of Architecture from the Yale School of Architecture and Herscovitch her BA in Architecture, Magna

Cum Laude, from Yale University. As faculty at Art Center College of Design, they were awarded the 2007 Nuckolls Fund for Lighting Education Grant. They have co-led international educational collaborations for Art Center, including the 2007 and 2012 Pacific Rim Projects in Tokyo in partnership with Tama Art University; and the award-winning Safe Agua project, initiated in 2009 between Art Center's Designmatters and the Innovation Center of N.G.O. TECHO to design innovative water solutions for Latin American communities with no running water.

J. Scott Hewit is an associate professor of education at Rollins College in Winter Park, FL. He has worked with the Rwandan Education Assistance Project (REAP) in Rwanda since 2010. His Rollins Laptop Legacy Project has resulted in some 30 refurbished laptops being brought to the rural Duha Complex School since 2011.

Lina Lee received her PhD from University of Texas, Austin. She is a professor of Spanish at the University of New Hampshire, where she teaches courses in second language acquisition, applied linguistics, and foreign language methodology. She has conducted research and published articles on language assessment, online feedback, computer-mediated communication, and discourse analysis.

Dr. Maysoun Dimachkie Masri is an assistant professor at the Department of Health Management and Informatics at the University of Central Florida. As a junior healthcare finance and economics researcher, Dr. Masri has worked on projects trying to delineate the causal relationship between efficiency and effectiveness of healthcare services. The focus of her research is directly related to the following disciplines: healthcare finance, healthcare finance education, economics, and healthcare policy.

 **Kathryn Mendez** earned her MA in Spanish from Middlebury College and is currently working toward a doctoral degree in Hispanic and Luso Brazilian Literatures and Languages from the CUNY Graduate Center in New York City. She is a Spanish teacher at the Hopkins School in New Haven, CT. Mendez has published poetry both in the United States and abroad, and she has most recently published literary criticism on the topic of Orientalism in Latin America.

 **Dr. Eunice M. Merideth** is the associate dean and a Levitt Distinguished Professor in the Drake University School of Education. She has designed and taught courses with and about technology for 24 years at the university level and worked with technology integration at all levels of education. In addition to being associate dean, Dr. Merideth is the assessment officer and LiveText coordinator for the Drake School of Education at Drake University, integrating a variety of technology assessment functions for the past 7 years. Dr. Merideth has also published two books and 44 articles on a range of educational topics, including educational technology, teacher leadership, educational equity, and instructional methodology.

Abigail Bragg New is a graduate of Rollins College in Winter Park, FL. She has taught in a Title 1 school that serves some of the poorest populations in downtown Orlando for the past 8 years. New has worked with REAP since 2012. She has assisted in establishing one of the first libraries in rural Rwanda and raised money to outfit the handball team at the Duha Complex School.

Bernardo Ramirez, MD, MBA, is an assistant professor and director of the Executive Master in Science in Health Services Administration Program (e-MSHSA) and of Global Health Initiatives of the Department of Health Management and Informatics at the University of Central Florida. Dr. Ramirez is an experienced health-services administrator in public and private organizations, and his experience includes clinical practice and administrative experience from the hospital departmental level to the health systems planning and policy levels. He has provided technical assistance, developed research, and conducted training for organizations including the U.S. Agency for International Development, the World Health Organization, and the W.K. Kellogg Foundation for 35 years in more than 60 countries on five continents. He has taught online courses atUCF since 2006 and is the author of numerous publications and training materials and a presenter at many national and international forums.

Dr. Cherie Lynn Ramirez is a Post-doctoral Fellow at the Harvard School of Public Health, with a joint appointment as Curriculum Fellow at the Harvard Global Health Institute. Her focus is primarily on priorities in the arena of education, including the development and implementation of a strategy to build a cadre of teaching fellows for global health courses, inclusive of teaching workshops in partnership with the Derek Bok Center for Teaching and Learning, teaching tools that can be shared across classes at Harvard, and a common set of resources that could be made available and accessible as educational public goods. She completed her PhD in experimental pathology through the Division of Medical Sciences at Harvard University in 2012. She holds an Associate in Arts degree from Valencia College and a Bachelor of Arts degree in classical studies and biochemistry/molecular biology from Rollins College. Dr. Ramirez has found her experiences living in Mexico, Spain, and Belgium and traveling extensively within the United States and abroad to be among her most enriching catalysts for learning and inspiration.

Carrie Schulz received her MBA from Crummer Graduate School of Business. She has served in a multitude of positions within the IT field and is currently the director of academic computing for Rollins College. During her career, she has embarked on multiple service immersions with students, bringing technology to schools in various forms. Her main focus of research is in bridging the digital divide and, more specifically, investigating how technology affects the quality of education that students receive.

Dr. Brian Shmaefsky is currently a professor of biology at Lone Star College, Kingwood, near Houston, and coordinates the college's service-learning program. He has been at the college since 1992. His research emphasis is in environmental physiology. Dr. Shmaefsky attended Brooklyn College of CUNY, Southern Illinois University at Edwardsville, Rocky Mountain Biological Laboratory, and University of Illinois. Currently, he is president of the Society for College Science Teachers and is active in other professional science and science education organizations. Dr. Shmaefsky also has done many presentations on higher education in the sciences and consults on environmental policy and scientific public education. He is the author of many peer-reviewed journal articles, has written several books on human disease and medicine, and authored a human anatomy and physiology textbook. Dr. Shmaefsky also serves on international organizations and governing boards with natural resource conservation and sustainability missions. He is the recipient of several teaching awards from his institution and from the American Association for the Advancement of Science, EXXON, the National Association of Biology Teachers, and the National Institute for Staff & Organizational Development. Dr. Shmaefsky lives in Kingwood with his wife, Julana, and her children Betsy, Josey, and Peter. His two children, Kathleen and Timothy, live nearby.

Dr. Peggy E. Steinbronn is an instructional designer for AEA PD Online, a statewide system for delivering online professional development to K–12 educators. In addition, she is an adjunct faculty member at Drake University School of Education, teaching technology integration and electronic portfolio courses for preservice teachers. Dr. Steinbronn has 27 years of K–12 classroom experience and 13 years teaching at the university level and has published extensively about technology in education.

About the Editors

Les Lloyd received his BS in Interdisciplinary Science and MBA from Rensselaer Polytechnic Institute. He has managed IT operations at Drew University, Lafayette College, Rollins College, and Saint Leo University, and he has published several books on higher-ed IT management and the use of technology in education.

Dr. Gabriel Ignacio Barreneche, associate professor of Spanish, received his BA in Spanish and International Studies from Boston College in 1996 after participating in that institution's study abroad program at the Universidad de San Francisco de Quito, Ecuador, during his junior year. He holds an MA and a PhD in Hispanic Languages and  Literatures from the University of California, Los Angeles. Since completing his graduate studies in 2003, Dr. Barreneche has been a member of the faculty of the Department of Modern Languages and Literatures at Rollins College in Winter Park, FL. He has published articles and presented papers on contemporary Caribbean and Latin American literature, Latino writers in the United States, service-learning pedagogy in the field of language instruction, and the role of instructional technology in language education.

Index

A